D0190839

INCLUDING THE EXCL

From practice to policy in
European community development

Paul Henderson

First published in Great Britain in June 2005 by

The Policy Press
University of Bristol
Fourth Floor
Beacon House
Queen's Road
Bristol BS8 1QU
UK

Tel +44 (0)117 331 4054
Fax +44 (0)117 331 4093
e-mail tpp-info@bristol.ac.uk
www.policypress.org.uk

Figure 4.1 is reproduced by kind permission of Oxford University Press.

British Library Cataloguing in Publication Data
A catalogue record for this book is available from the British Library.

Library of Congress Cataloging-in-Publication Data
A catalog record for this book has been requested.

ISBN 978 186134 745 9 paperback

Paul Henderson is a community development consultant and a Visiting Professor at De Montfort University, Leicester, UK.

Cover design by Qube Design Associates, Bristol.
Front cover: photograph supplied by kind permission of www.third-avenue.co.uk.
Printed and bound in Great Britain by Athenaeum Press, Gateshead.

Contents

Foreword

The continuing existence of political, economic and social barriers that prevent millions of people across Europe from participating fully in society is being challenged by a range of groups and organisations. The expansion of the European Union (EU) from 370 million to nearly 450 million people in May 2004 has required groups and organisations to redouble their efforts: most of the new citizens are significantly poorer than those from the former EU.

The focus of *Including the excluded* is on actions taken by community groups across Europe. It has been prepared and written on a collaborative basis by individuals who are closely involved in working on the issue. Critical to the publication's authenticity has been the involvement of activists and community development workers in Norway, Sweden, Belgium, England and Spain. It is their voices that have informed the writing and, on behalf of the Combined European Bureau for Social Development (CEBSD), I would like to thank them for their support.

CEBSD is a small European network playing a key role through the breadth of its activities and its capacity to keep in contact with grassroots action. It depends heavily on informal contacts and the willingness of its member organisations to contribute time and energy. In the case of this publication, two of the members have made specific contributions: the Combat Poverty Agency by way of a grant towards the costs of producing the book, and the Community Development Foundation through its support for the involvement of Paul Henderson in the project. I would like to thank both organisations.

The issues of poverty and social exclusion are far from being new, but they have acquired new dimensions. Furthermore the mechanisms and tools available to address social exclusion have developed: national and European programmes, research findings, the work of non-governmental and campaigning organisations, networks and community groups. CEBSD believes that this publication will help to sustain the action being undertaken by local, regional, national and European community development organisations on the issue of social exclusion. CEBSD is committed to supporting the activities of its members and others in this process. It also seeks to inform and influence policies of the EU and the member states about effective, community-based strategies for combating social exclusion.

Gerard Hautekeur (Chair, CEBSD)

Acknowledgements

I wish to thank all those people who were involved in the community development and social exclusion project undertaken by CEBSD. I am particularly grateful to those people who wrote the case studies for this publication. I could not have asked for more support than that given to me by CEBSD's Board and Margo Gorman (coordinator) during the process of preparing and completing the book. My thanks to Harry Salmon for commenting on the final draft.

Paul Henderson

ONE

Beginnings

The issue of language has a special irony for this publication: people's experiences of poverty, exclusion, homelessness, unemployment and many other pressures on their lives are mostly stark and direct – not obscure. 'Social exclusion', 'transparency', 'capacity building', 'indicators' – what meaning do these and other terms have for most people? Community activists and other members of community groups and associations are increasingly frustrated by the jargon that is so dominant in policy documents and strategy papers: 'officialese', buzzwords, acronyms, abbreviations, overcomplicated sentences. The very people who are the victims of social exclusion are thus hindered from challenging it because of the language used by others.

In what follows, we have sought to avoid the same trap. We aim to demystify and clarify the concepts and principles that are used by both policy makers and practitioners when they seek to work with neighbourhood groups and communities of interest. Above all, we set out to communicate key messages about how neighbourhoods, communities and networks mobilise and organise around the issue of social exclusion. Many of the ideas and 'good practice' lessons come from work undertaken jointly by groups of people in several European countries. How this came about is explained later in this chapter. First, however, we specify the book's objectives as follows:

- to capture the shared experiences and principles of a range of people involved in community development across Europe;
- to specify the contribution of community development to combating social exclusion;
- to communicate 'good practice' lessons from communities that are engaged with the issue of social exclusion;
- to suggest how governments, local authorities, non-governmental organisations and partnerships can support communities that are experiencing and taking action on social exclusion.

The member organisations of the Combined European Bureau for Social Development (CEBSD) are national or regional organisations that support and promote community development. Through their own members, networks and projects they have contact with a range of organisations and groups, including those working at the grassroots. The material that follows draws primarily on action and ideas coming from this level. It makes connections with other levels – local authorities, government agencies, research institutions – but its central concern is with what does and does not work for local people, especially those who are experiencing social exclusion and who are involved in community development and community action.

The book has been written for those people who are involved at grassroots level: community leaders, community development workers and other community-based professionals (for example youth workers, health staff, economic development officers); the managers and policy makers of organisations that are committed to supporting grassroots action; those who are responsible for training programmes; European policy makers and non-governmental organisations and networks.

Definitions

The meanings of many of the terms used in this book are the subject of lively debate, not least the term 'social exclusion'. The extent to which this concept has become established within European policy and practice dialogues is welcome. There are disagreements about what the term means, but it offers "a more comprehensive, multi-dimensional understanding than traditional formulations of poverty" (Lister, 2004, p 92). It is used in this publication to refer to people who are prevented from participating fully in society because of poverty, discrimination and lack of opportunities. 'Inclusion' is used sometimes instead of the more negative 'exclusion'. In Scotland, at the time that the term was being introduced, 'social exclusion' was seen by many people as being divisive and discriminatory and there was a clear preference for policies based on the principle of social inclusion. Levitas (1998) has pointed out that the use of words such as 'exclusion' and 'inclusion' can hide the extent of inequalities and can encourage the view that all that is required is more opportunity for everyone and marginal shifts of money to those who are poorest. She also identifies "three discourses of social exclusion". The first is based on the redistribution of wealth and is concerned mainly with poverty, the second is based on the notion of an 'underclass' and the third is based on social integration, concentrates on paid work and contains a mixture of opportunities and coercion. Levitas illustrates the way in which politicians' definitions of social exclusion move uneasily between any two or even all three interpretations. In this publication, 'social exclusion' is given a broad meaning, encompassing all key aspects of people's lives in communities, not simply whether or not they join or rejoin the labour market.

Unlike the word 'poverty', social exclusion encourages a focus on process – how and why people are prevented from participating in society – rather than simply outcomes or results. This places the concept of social inclusion very close to that of community development (or social development). That social exclusion is a dynamic rather than a static concept means that it can be used flexibly. It also means that recognition is given to the interaction between various elements of social exclusion. For example, acquiring a vocational skill or even getting a job does not necessarily end the condition of exclusion, and not all people in poverty live in the poorest areas. The idea of people being trapped in a 'web' of social exclusion is discussed in Henderson and Salmon (2001, pp 15-23).

An interesting example of how close community development is to social inclusion comes from an action-research project on community care. The project worked in four communities in Scotland with local people, practitioners and local authority staff to study the contribution that community development could make to caring for vulnerable people in communities, particularly elderly people and people with disabilities:

> The experience of the projects was that, from a community and service user perspective, issues relating specifically to community care services could not be conveniently isolated from many others that determined the quality of personal or community life. Exclusion was a powerful common denominator between care users and others in the community. Needs were consistently placed in a context that connected them to wider community concerns related, for example, to transport, safety, planning, leisure opportunities, accessible services or responsive governance. (Barr et al, 2001, p 5)

Community development is the process of change that takes place in communities with the active involvement of local people: "Community development is distinguished from social work and allied welfare professions through its commitment to collective ways of addressing problems. Community development helps community members to identify unmet needs, to undertake research on the problems and present possible solutions" (Gilchrist, 2004b, p 21). This author goes on to remind us that there are different models of community development, each related to contrasting political analyses of society and the state. Community development is a concept on which strong opinions are held.

Community groups and networks are the lifeblood of community development. Whether formally constituted or not, they are characterised by people cooperating and organising together. Community action is when groups or networks set out to achieve certain objectives. Community groups consist entirely of volunteers and the number of groups that employ a community development worker is very small. This contrasts with local, regional, national and European voluntary organisations or non-governmental organisations, the majority of which do employ staff.

Community workers have been active in deprived neighbourhoods for many years. Their work has been based on a set of values that can be summarised as follows:

- Local people have a right to be consulted about decisions that affect their area.
- Involvement in community groups and networks is entirely voluntary.
- Local people should be supported in achieving their goals, provided that these are not discriminatory.
- The pace of the change process should be determined by the participants and not by the needs or priorities of external organisations.

A problem for community development when seeking to engage with local people on the issue of social exclusion can be that some poor people do not wish to be identified as such. Research on rural social exclusion in Scotland, for example, reported:

> The most challenging finding of the research on disadvantage in rural Scotland was that rural people's own assessment was at odds with official definitions of poverty. Most looked back on the improvements since their own childhood, when they lacked running water, electricity and TVs, and could not conceive of themselves as poor. (Shucksmith, 2000, p 15)

A skilled community worker should be able to handle this kind of situation. More serious are research findings indicating that some people with current experience of poverty can object to the use of the word 'poverty'. Ruth Lister points out that "the adjective 'poor' is also tainted by its double meaning of inferior, as in 'poor quality' or 'deficient'. Its use as an adjective can be experienced as insulting and demeaning" (Lister, 2004, p 113).

The term 'statutory organisation' is used to refer to local authorities, health boards, regional agencies and other bodies that have been established under the auspices of the state. The term 'private sector organisation' describes profit-making companies and corporations. Increasingly all of these types of organisation come together in local or regional partnerships in order to work together on regeneration and community-based programmes.

The project

The work undertaken for *Including the excluded* draws on a range of knowledge and experiences both among the member organisations of CEBSD and other networks, especially those that have a commitment to making the connections between community development and social exclusion. Discussions and exchanges of information across Europe – and beyond – are continuing. In March 2004, CEBSD, the Hungarian Association for Community Development and the International Association for Community Development organised a conference in Budapest that reaffirmed the importance of articulating the community development dimension of struggles to strengthen civil society and combat social exclusion. Thus the practice and principles that are captured in this publication are part of a wider, continuing dialogue and debate. They are not looking back. Nor are they merely setting out an overoptimistic ideal. Quite the reverse: they are rooted in the realities of people's lives in community settings, in the knowledge that the realities are constantly subject to unanticipated pressures and changes.

The starting point for the project, and the main source of the good practice principles discussed here, was a specific programme of action and reflection undertaken in 2002-03 by CEBSD and partner organisations. It formed part of the first phase of the European Union's (EU's) Community Action Programme on Social Exclusion, which was launched in 2002. Five member organisations of CEBSD in Norway, Sweden, Belgium, England and Spain formed a partnership. In Oslo, Orebro, Ghent, Bradford and Barcelona, working groups were set up consisting of community members/volunteers, community development workers, local authority staff, researchers and policy makers. The working groups held several meetings that had two purposes: to analyse examples of community development practice focused on social inclusion and to clarify guiding principles according to shared guidelines. There was a CEBSD representative on each group and usually he or she took the lead role in documenting the work and writing it up. The experiences and findings of the groups were shared at each stage of the project and brought together by a transnational planning group. The process culminated at a seminar in Berlin at which the working groups presented their results and where the participants achieved a high level of agreement on good practice principles. A report on the project was submitted to the European Commission (Gorman, 2003).

Several of the working groups continued to meet after the project had finished. Furthermore, other members and contacts of CEBSD became involved and contact was made with other projects in the EU programme. This sharing of experience indicates increasing recognition of the role of community development in helping to support economic development, regeneration and social inclusion.

As a result of the commitment to continue the work begun by the good practice project, CEBSD remains deeply involved with the issues. It is supporting contact between community development workers and members of community groups across Europe intent on clarifying and illustrating effective ways of using community development to tackle social exclusion. It is also taking forward plans to build up the learning, on a Europe–wide basis, of community development responses to social exclusion.

It is essential to place the principles and practice of community development explored in this book within the wider European context, and this is the focus of Chapter Two. In order to demonstrate the kinds of interventions and initiatives that combine community development and social inclusion, we give summaries in Chapter Three of the case studies presented at the Berlin seminar. The studies have been updated and finalised in collaboration with members of the working groups. We also include case studies from Hungary and Denmark. In Chapter Four, we lay out the shared principles that have been drawn both from the practice examples and other experiences, seeking to specify key factors required for effective community development in the context of social exclusion. In Chapter Five, we address the question: Do the organisations that use and promote community development in different parts of Europe have a common understanding of what the term means, particularly in relation to social exclusion? CEBSD considered that it was essential to discuss this question because of the need to ensure that we are working on a European issue that is genuinely shared: action at a local level has to relate to a coherent European understanding of community development. Chapter Six addresses the question of what community development and other organisations can do to strengthen the case for a community development approach to social exclusion. It includes a case study from Ireland about policy change at the European level. Any action agenda on social exclusion should not simply be a manifesto or a list of requests. It should be based on important, exciting developments in communities across Europe that face severe economic, social and environmental problems and where too many members of communities are experiencing social exclusion in one form or another. It must be an agenda, therefore, that has implications as much for policy makers and politicians as it does for practitioners and local people. It is crucial to overcome the hurdles that make communication and joint work with a range of actors or partners so challenging in the European context.

In a concluding chapter, we reflect more generally on community development itself and highlight key points that emerge from the previous chapters. This gives a signal that the need for work to be undertaken within community development organisations is as pressing as the need to engage with other organisations and with European policy issues.

TWO

The European context

European policy and practice take place in a dynamic and changing context. The development of key concepts regarding this context has to take the complexity of these social, political and economic changes into account. Further, Europe is not self-contained and free of the impact of wider global interactions and exchanges. Learning from wider international sources is especially important when discussing social exclusion and community development. Many individuals and organisations in the North have learned from approaches taken in the South to address and tackle poverty and related concerns: the use, for example, of participatory research and evaluation methods and inspiring examples of sustained community development and campaigning.

Among a wide range of policy makers and politicians in Europe there is a growing awareness that the state has to be active in the sphere of community in addition to its responsibilities to and for individuals and families. This aspect is evidenced more widely too. Political scientists have supplied politicians and policy makers with information on the low voting patterns of citizens in many local and some national elections (Dalton and Wattenberg, 2000). They have also documented feelings of the disillusionment of voters with politicians and political parties as well as the influence of campaigning international social movements and organisations. More far-sighted politicians have taken these messages seriously and have been prepared to recognise and support initiatives that encourage participatory democracy to flourish alongside representative democracy.

The purpose of this chapter is to draw attention to these and related themes and concepts and to demonstrate how these aspects of the European context reach out to communities, community development and European policies. In this way, the scene will be set for understanding the more focused material discussed in the subsequent chapters. First, however, it is important to draw out the concepts and theories that relate most powerfully to communities and community development.

Civil society

The emergence of civil society as a concept that, across the globe, underpins expressions of popular movements and community action has been remarkable. It is a term that crosses borders and cultures with apparent ease, although a number of commentators have pointed to the varied and changing meanings attached to it. Jensen and Miszlivetz (2003) for example, in a wide-ranging review of the concept, come down in favour of an approach that uses civil society as a metaphor – an "aspirational usage" (p 82).

The concept of civil society, so central at the time of the revolutions in Eastern and Central Europe, has continued to exercise a powerful influence on political discourse as it relates to non-governmental organisations and communities. This gives out an essentially positive message about the scope for peaceful change – despite manifestations of racism and anti-democratic forces in different parts of Europe: "The longterm growth of European-wide exchanges among civilians whose social and political views are predominantly pluralist and democratic is among the most remarkable – and least remarked on – features of contemporary Europe" (Keane, 1998, pp 112-13). One of the reasons for the continuing significance of the concept of civil society is to be found in the importance of autonomous, grassroots organisations in community development thinking. Civil society and community development are, in that sense, part of the same dialogue. Speaking at a Central–Eastern European seminar, Ilona Vercseg of the Hungarian Association for Community Development stated: "The emergence and development of community development and community work as a professional field shows that this profession can directly be linked to democracy and the emergence of civil society" (Vercseg, 2003).

The struggle for genuine democracy within Europe is driven by grassroots, campaigning organisations and trades unions, supported by European non-governmental organisations and networks. It is possible, however, for governments to take initiatives too. The Swedish government set up a Commission on Swedish Democracy and, in 2000, launched a project called Time for Democracy aimed at promoting democracy and supporting active citizen participation: "There is a particular focus on local democracy, schools and groups that at present play relatively little part in the development of society" (Ministry of Justice, 2002, p 2).

In addition to being part of debates among citizens and within community development organisations, and between them and governments, the significance of civil society is recognised within

European policy making. In the EU, the provisional version of the treaty establishing a European constitution includes a commitment to the principle of participatory democracy: "The Institutions shall maintain an open, transparent and regular dialogue with representative associations and civil society" (EU, 2004, p 60). Alongside its commitment to building civil society, the European Commission is increasingly aware of the challenges this poses:

> If civil society is to be fully engaged in the development of policies at European and national levels this can only be truly successful if it is built on the solid base of a vibrant civil society at local level. The problem, of course, is that where there is extensive poverty and social exclusion, deep-seated inequality or discrimination then civil society is likely to be weakened. (Frazer, 2005: forthcoming)

Social capital

The research and writings of Robert Putnam and others on social capital have had a high profile in recent years. Putnam carried out research, first in Italy and then in the US, showing a relationship between the social and community infrastructure of a society and economic development. Social capital refers both to networks and trust between people, and to the relationship between people and institutions. It can be highly significant in building strong communities.

Brian Harvey has suggested that, in looking for evidence of social capital in excluded communities, we may be looking for the following features:

- communities that decide, behave and involve people inclusively in an egalitarian way with respect for cultural diversity;
- communities that develop links to like-minded groups, the systems of governance and intermediary bodies (these processes may be called bonding, linking and bridging social capital);
- communities with a high level of social cohesion, identity, belonging, trust and sense of purpose;
- communities in the course of developing their human resources, capacities and leadership;
- attitudinal change in communities, with a growing trust of local, regional and national systems of governance;

- behavioural change in communities, showing growing levels of associational activity, volunteering, membership and engagement. (Harvey, 2003, p 8)

The emphasis of social capital theory on trust and cooperation explains why the concept has been received positively by many people involved in community development. It provides a theoretical underpinning that, while remaining contested, is contemporary and applicable globally. Social capital also connects strongly with the practice of community development:

- It is only possible to work effectively with local people when there is a baseline of trust and willingness to cooperate. The early stages of community development are frequently almost entirely focused on achieving a minimal level of mutual trust between people as well as the potential for cooperation.
- Community development practice sets out to respond to situations where there are weak or perhaps neglected notions of social capital; its interest is in bringing people together, first into informal groups and then more formal organisations. This is about building social capital.
- At different stages in the community development process, local leaders will be important in terms of representing the interest of community groups. Community workers will often spend time with such people, encouraging them to increase their self-confidence and skills. This, therefore, is another way in which community development connects with social capital.

Other disciplines, particularly public health and community economic development, have shown strong interest in the concept – a 1997 World Bank report on defining and measuring social capital refers to it as the 'missing link' in the development process. Alison Gilchrist suggests that community cohesion programmes, which are designed to respond to situations in communities of conflict and fragmentation, can be guided by the concept of social capital: "[it] provides a useful way of thinking about community cohesion in terms of the connections and associations that exist between people, groups and communities" (Gilchrist, 2004a, p 12).

Capacity building

The term 'capacity building' originated in the US but increasingly it is being incorporated into European, governmental and local authority policies. It emphasises a systematic approach towards helping residents play a major part in the regeneration of their communities. It is:

> Development work that strengthens the ability of community organisations and groups to build their own structures, systems, people and skills so that they are better able to define and achieve their objectives and engage in consultation and planning, manage community projects and take part in partnerships and community enterprises. It includes aspects of training, organisational and personal development and resource building, organised in a planned and self-conscious manner, reflecting the principles of empowerment and equality. (Skinner, 1997, pp 1-2)

While capacity building is concerned mainly with the activities of community groups and voluntary organisations, it also needs to form an essential part of developing the skills and knowledge of staff in statutory organisations – local authorities, health agencies, planning organisations and so on. Frequently it is because staff in these organisations are not sufficiently equipped to work in and with communities that working relationships between them and local people fail. In the UK, a government review of community capacity building recognises the centrality of community development values and skills. The first priority for action specified in the review report is "the development of a much more comprehensive and coherent menu of learning opportunities for community engagement, both for citizens and communities, *and for professionals, practitioners and policy makers*" (Civil Renewal Unit, 2004, p 3; emphasis added).

Community capacity building can be seen to form part of the tradition of learning and community education within community development. Community workers place a high priority on there being training and education opportunities that are accessible to members of community groups. Arguably, such opportunities are essential for achieving the sustainability of regeneration and social inclusion programmes. They are opportunities, furthermore, that relate to debates on poverty, specifically to the idea of 'capabilities', the kind of life that a person is able to lead and the choices and opportunities open to him or her in leading that life: "the freedom people enjoy to choose between different ways of living that they can have reason to value" (Sen, 1990, p 114). Ruth Lister points out that capability theorists focus on the positive, the kind of life people may want to achieve, rather than the negative – the lack of material resources that can prevent them from achieving it (Lister, 2004, p 17). This can have the effect of moving poverty out of a self-contained box and of linking it with other concerns within society.

The links between community development and capacity building are strong. The latter term is used in other, mainly organisational, contexts across Europe. Its potential relevance to combating social exclusion, through the provision of a range of accessible learning opportunities, has still to be fully realised.

Communities

Is it meaningful to think about communities in the European context? Indeed, is it possible to put forward any valid generalisations about 'community' any more? Sociologists have written strongly on the extent to which it is a 'contested concept', one on which it is inherently difficult to reach agreement. Bauman, for example, states that 'community' is now another name for paradise lost: "'Community' stands for the kind of world which is not, regrettably, available to us – but which we would dearly wish to inhabit and which we hope to repossess" (Bauman, 2001, p 3). Yet community is a concept with which community development workers and others have to engage day by day. Indeed, it is unlikely that they would be involved in community development unless they were deeply interested in understanding communities and how they work. They have to try and make sense of community and to keep pace with its changing meanings.

The experience of most local people and community development workers who have opportunities to share their thinking and practice within a European framework is that comparisons between communities are possible. Perhaps precisely because every community is distinctive, even unique, it is possible to gain insights and understanding. This was certainly, as we shall see, what participants in CEBSD's project discovered.

If we hold in our minds a definition of 'community' that embraces locality, common interests and shared identity, we can identify some patterns within Europe:

- A *sense of oppression* characterises many disadvantaged communities. This is certainly true for minority ethnic groups such as the Roma because of the discrimination they experience. It applies also, however, to some rural communities, which have been neglected for many years by government agencies and which may either be geographically isolated or still experiencing the poverty and disruption caused by industrial decline – closure of coal mines, for example, in the UK, Belgium, France and Hungary.
- *Poverty and unemployment.* These are the two major issues facing many people in deprived communities. There are considerable variations between countries. In the Czech Republic, for example, the risk of poverty is 8% while in Estonia it is 18%. However, it is the concentrations of high levels of poverty and unemployment that are critical to understanding the European context of community development and social exclusion. Neglected public housing estates, inner-city areas and isolated rural communities experience the worst of these problems.
- *High levels of conflict.* This is especially apparent in densely populated areas and in communities in which there is minimal contact and understanding between different cultures, faiths and ethnic groups. A degraded environment can exacerbate conflict: poorly maintained housing blocks, lack of security, open drug dealing, vandalism and graffiti. But covert forms of conflict can exist in other communities, even in some rural communities where relatively affluent 'incomers' are not integrated with long-established residents.
- *A sense of isolation* characterises many of the communities where community development takes place. It often stems from neglect by public agencies. This then leads to an intuition among residents that promises made by agencies will be broken – nothing works.
- *Insecurity, high levels of crime and the dominance of fear of crime* are to be found in the most excluded communities. This applies to inner-city neighbourhoods and public housing estates, less often to rural communities.
- *Poor facilities* – for example a lack of good quality playgrounds and community centres.
- *Under-resourced and unreliable public services* – for example too few social workers, youth workers, health visitors.

This list underlines the reality that multiple strands of exclusion come together in the most disadvantaged neighbourhoods. This analysis can hold true also for some communities of interest and identity such as refugees. The phrase 'out of sight, out of mind' is appropriate: the dominant majority society in Western Europe is relatively wealthy and it is not difficult for its members to assume that everyone is in a similar position to themselves, to be oblivious to the polarisation and inequality so close to them. Turn one way out of Brussels central station and one enters a lively, well-maintained environment; turn the other way – into the northern section of the city – and a different world is visible. This kind of analysis can be applied to different social and spatial contexts, from urban neighbourhoods in cities to small towns and remote rural areas. It can also be used to understand the situations of particular groupings in society, for example of disabled people, children and young people. Common to all of these situations and groups is their separateness from mainstream society. As a consequence, they are prevented from participating fully in society.

We must be careful, however, not to fall into the trap of painting an entirely negative, despairing picture of communities dominated by social exclusion: an arithmetic of woe in which exclusion, poverty and deprivation are equated with loss of community. That would be very misleading. Again and again community development workers and others provide evidence of the resilience of such communities. They face many inter-related problems and they need to be strengthened. Often, however, they have characteristics that can be the envy of richer, cleaner, more modern neighbourhoods:

- *resourcefulness* – the capacity to draw on individual and collective forms of self-help in, for example, setting up enterprises;
- *informal networks and social ties,* which equip people to act effectively in public arenas. The role of women is particularly important here;
- *mutual aid* – people helping each other as a natural part of living in a community. This is especially apparent in some rural areas;
- *diversity* – the positive aspects of multiracial, multicultural communities and the richness that can result from this. In contrast are 'gated' communities of the well-off in which there is a poverty of human contact with people who are different.

The quality of life in neighbourhoods matters to local people, even if their neighbourhoods have been categorised as having high levels of social exclusion and low levels of social capital: "To the extent that dense webs of relationships, trust and familiarity constitute an important dimension of social capital these areas have rich resources to draw on" (Forrest and Kearns, 1999, p 22).

Community development workers and organisations have to work with these contradictory messages about Europe's disadvantaged communities. They walk a tightrope between, on the one hand, exposing the problems and suffering facing these communities and, on the other hand, drawing attention to the strengths they have. The bottom line, however, has to do with the strengths and weaknesses of groups and organisations in these communities. It is these resources, linked to networks and capacity building opportunities, that can lead to communities gaining greater control over decisions and resources, and it is these that are the crucial ingredients for building stronger communities.

In Northern Ireland the term 'community infrastructure' has been coined to refer to this dimension of social and economic change. It is used in order to obtain an understanding of the phenomena of 'weak' and 'strong' communities. Between 1996 and 2000, the Community Foundation for Northern Ireland undertook a mapping exercise of areas considered to have weak community infrastructures. It defined these as areas that were isolated, lacked previous development, did not have community venues or resources, lacked leadership, where there was little associational activity, were neglected by government, were characterised by community division and suffered from social deprivation (see O'Prey and Magowan, 2001). 'Developing community infrastructure' became a measure in the Peace 11 of the EU's Peace and Reconciliation Programme. The Rural Community Network (Northern Ireland) initiated a programme in 13 cluster areas. It includes early capacity building work and employs 13 development workers. 'Mapping' the infrastructural weaknesses of very deprived communities and then building or rebuilding their social capital are of central importance in specifying the contribution of community development to tackling social exclusion.

Community development

Tracing the connections between how communities organise themselves and community development has become increasingly important. One reason for this is that many communities have experienced more than 30 years of community development interventions. Particularly in the UK, France, the Netherlands and Flanders and Brussels in Belgium, there has been a succession of government-funded programmes designed to support and work in partnership with communities. Whatever the successes and failures of these programmes, local residents have become more knowledgeable about them and about community development. They have been at the receiving end of community development and have learnt from this.

The positive aspect of this has been the willingness of experienced activists to take leading roles in the process of strengthening their communities. Most of these people have been women. This comment by an activist who went on to train and practise as a community worker is typical of the commitment shown by women to their communities:

> The end results in the campaign were that local people believed they had won a long hard battle and the real work to make the changes in the community had just begun. I believe many 'community champions' were born during this time, with leading activists who were confident to express themselves to both local and national governments in their 'fight' for their homes.
>
> These were mostly women who inspired their community through community action.... I witnessed many people develop the confidence to 'take on the world' after the campaign.... Many saw their involvement as a short-term campaign, whilst many others tried hard to move into the next campaign that would benefit both themselves and the community as a whole. Those who slipped into the community development process are, more than a decade later, still fully active in their community groups.... Another successful development was the active involvement of some local women who liberated themselves by braving the challenges of participating on residential training courses at Northern College in Barnsley, South Yorkshire. I know how successful this feels as I am one of those women. (Cousins, 2005, pp 6-7)

In addition to becoming skilled community leaders, some local activists have begun to undertake tasks in communities that traditionally would have been undertaken by community development workers. Significant numbers, like those in the community action example above, have made extensive use of local and regional opportunities for learning about communities, community development and politics.

Evidence for the development of 'change from the inside' is to be found in the survey of community development workers in the UK undertaken in 2001-02. The survey included a pilot study of local people who were 'unpaid community workers'. The study found that it was difficult to distinguish between 'doing' in the community (roles traditionally associated with unpaid activists and volunteers) and the enabling and facilitating roles more likely to be associated with paid community development workers. From the interviews with the unpaid workers, four clear areas of activity emerged where interviewees had adopted roles typical of community development methods and similar to those taken by paid workers. These were:

- empowering and supporting individuals' involvement;
- enabling the development of new and existing groups;
- identifying issues and promoting involvement in governance;
- building networks and links in the community.

If we take the second of these roles, not only did interviewees with long experience of doing community work adopt development roles in supporting groups, they were also consciously experimenting with the methods they were using:

> With this residents' group, I am using all the experience I have had for the last 25 years in nurturing a group of people to form a coherent effective group. I am evolving a strategy for seeing if I can grow a different kind of residents' group with the objective of being able to get out with the thing going well. It's based on building absolute personal relationships bit by bit as the root ... so that we don't fall over ... if it grows strong enough it can be a real community group, but it can't start by doing that. (Glen et al, 2004, p 48)

There may be a reservoir of people in communities who have acquired skills traditionally seen as the domain of professional workers. This does not mean that the role of professional community development workers would become redundant but rather that the role would change. It is a trend that becomes manifest in different ways according to the national, regional and cultural context. From its inception, for example, the Hungarian Association for Community Development sought to encourage local people to train as community development workers. In Barcelona, there are striking examples of local activists taking on new responsibilities in cultural mediation and arts projects.

In the wider context, the idea of 'change from the inside' gives an important signal about the dynamism of community development. Its history goes back many decades, and sometimes the literature that is available to learn about it seems in danger of having been left behind by the practice of community development and the responsiveness of communities both to major issues and to intervention programmes. By looking closely at what is happening at grassroots level in communities across Europe, it is possible to point to the energy and ideas existing in pressurised communities. This is of critical importance in wider discussions about civil society and social exclusion in Europe and it is vital for policy makers to be informed about it.

It is in order to have a means of taking the pulse of community development across Europe that CEBSD makes networking a priority between its members, learning from good practice and disseminating this. Staying close to the experiences of communities and community development workers is crucial for the organisation. Since its foundation in 1990, CEBSD has developed its networking role. It encourages joint work between its members: during the 1990s, for example, the Hungarian organisation worked closely with trainers in the UK on rural community development. CEBSD also seeks to link groups and organisations that are not members. In recent years, there have been several examples of this happening in Eastern and Central Europe, often with the financial support of organisations such as the Mott Foundation.

The other characteristic of the work carried out by CEBSD, its members and partners is the cross-cutting nature of community development in Europe. By this, we mean the way that, within a framework of community development, particular issues are prioritised in different countries. This in turn leads to other CEBSD members learning about an issue and taking it forward in their context.

At the level of practice, the cross-cutting theme reflects the holistic principle in community development, namely that local people tend not to separate out needs and issues according to one discipline or profession; they experience them as a cluster or related set – health, poverty, safety, environment are interconnected in the life of a community and they need to be addressed in that way. That is why community development works best when it has a generalist rather than a specialist remit.

Examples of particular themes or issues developed by one CEBSD member and built on by other members are:

- *Democracy* – this has been worked on intensively by the Centre for Community Work and Mobilisation (CESAM), the Swedish member. It has lead to visits and exchanges in Scotland and England

and a dialogue with the Hungarian Association for Community Development.

- *Civil society* – the key idea that underpins the thinking and work of the Hungarian organisation and the work undertaken by other community development organisations in Eastern and Central Europe. It is an idea that is discussed frequently within CEBSD.
- *Intercultural mediation* – a methodology developed by Desenvolupament Comunitari, CEBSD's member in Spain, to respond to situations of tension and conflict between communities. The topic has been the focus of two European conferences.
- *Regeneration* – the need for community development to form a key part of both urban and rural regeneration programmes has been a major theme in several Northern European countries, particularly the UK and the Netherlands. CEBSD has organised meetings and conferences on the issue.
- *Environmental action* – the importance of local community action on the issue of sustainable development and Local Agenda 21 has gained increased recognition. CEBSD's member in Norway, The Ideas Bank, has opened up the issue for other CEBSD members, using its experience in Norway to demonstrate the links with community development.
- *Social exclusion* – as a result of the project undertaken for the EU, this has become of central importance to CEBSD. Efforts are being made to specify the links with community development at the policy level as well as through practice. Much has been learned from the practice and policy work of the Combat Poverty Agency. In 2004, VIBOSO, the Flemish Institute for Community Development in Flanders and Brussels, organised a conference on the theme in the Flemish Parliament. It brought together representatives of the partner organisations involved in CEBSD's project.

The dissemination and exchange of good practice in community development within Europe has grown significantly in recent years. Much of it is achieved through networking and visits. The knowledge base that is growing complements information sources available on the Internet and through studies of particular issues. The Carnegie Commission for Rural Community Development, for example, commissioned a study of rural community development in Europe (Craig et al, 2004).

We look more closely at how community development is understood in different countries in Chapter Five. The overview given in this chapter demonstrates how its principles and practice have gained increased recognition in the European context.

Policy

In 1989, the Council of Europe's Standing Conference of Local and Regional Authorities of Europe passed a resolution on self-help and community development in towns. It acknowledged the work of international organisations, such as the United Nations and World Health Organization, on community development and urged local authorities to take forward and resource community development. However, it has been the EU that, over the last 15 years, has provided a more favourable context for community development.

With the exception of the EU Peace and Reconciliation Programme in Northern Ireland, the term 'community development' is not used by the EU. The language is more that of community involvement, participation, local development and partnership, and it is a language that relates strongly to employment and social inclusion. For example, those regions that have Objective One status, making them eligible for additional funding, are expected to set up and support partnerships that enable local people to be involved in decision making about the allocation of resources. For rural areas, the LEADER+ rural development programme also has an expectation that communities would be involved in local partnerships.

The EU's structural funds were reformed in the late 1980s "to make them more effective instruments in promoting balanced regional and social development. They have funded a number of actions touching on social capital, even if they have not been so named" (Harvey, 2003, p 9). The structural funds could have a key role to play in strengthening citizen involvement in local, regional and national development.

Why should the EU wish to support and promote community involvement? One reason has to do with control. By encouraging participation, deprived communities can become more integrated with the dominant values and norms of society. This was the primary meaning given to social exclusion in France, where the term originated in the 1970s. The attention given to community safety, as well as support for work with migrants and members of minority ethnic groups, are the most obvious examples of the control motive. An analysis of control and community development can be found in a special issue on Europe of the *Community Development Journal* (Tonkens and Duyvendak, 2003).

At the same time, we can see that policy makers are interested in 'community' and community involvement because they have become aware of the need to strengthen the idea of neighbourhood in regeneration and social inclusion programmes. Some policy makers also take the realistic approach: if communities are not involved, then the chances of programmes being effective are not high. Community groups need to be convinced that decisions made by large agencies and programmes about the future of their communities are authentic. They also need to feel a sense of ownership of changes that take place in their communities.

An idea that is attractive in the European policy context is that of social cohesion and it is an idea that connects strongly with the values of community development: seeking to help people to live and work together, to recognise differences and to find ways of strengthening communities. It is the EU's engagement with social exclusion, however, that provides greater potential for community development in the European context. The EU's work on poverty goes back 30 years to the pilot poverty programmes. Some of the projects, particularly those based in rural areas, developed a strong commitment to community development and it is important to recognise that more recent initiatives are building on this experience. The EU's Social Inclusion Programme was launched in 2002. This followed the agreement at the Lisbon European Council in 2000 to adopt an "open method of coordination" with the aim of "making a decisive impact on the eradication of poverty by 2010" (European Council, 2000, p 10). The key elements of this method are:

- setting common EU objectives for combating poverty and social exclusion;
- each member state drawing up its own national action plan against poverty and social exclusion;
- encouraging a process of mutual learning and dialogue between member states that will stimulate innovation and the sharing of best practice;
- agreeing and collecting data on a set of common indicators across the EU in order to compare policies and to measure progress in reducing poverty and social exclusion;
- involving all stakeholders in the process;
- putting in place arrangements to ensure the coordination of the process and regular monitoring and reporting on progress.

The common objectives of the Social Inclusion Programme are grouped around four major headings:

1. to promote participation in employment and access of all to resources, goods, services and rights;
2. to prevent poverty and social exclusion;
3. to support the most vulnerable;
4. to mobilise and involve all stakeholders.

The objective of mobilising all relevant bodies speaks directly to community development organisations: the need for dialogue with a range of organisations, including community groups. Hugh Frazer drew attention to this when addressing a community development audience:

> Amongst other things this emphasises promoting the participation and self-expression of people suffering social exclusion, in particular in regard to their situation and the policies and measures affecting them. It also stresses the promotion of dialogue and partnership between all relevant bodies, public and private, and emphasises the involvement of all social partners. In other words it puts civil society and especially those experiencing poverty and social exclusion at the heart of the process. (Frazer, 2005: forthcoming)

As the EU's Social Inclusion Programme develops, it will be vital for community development organisations to debate the findings. At the European level, this will require networks like CEBSD to work alongside other European non-governmental organisations and to speak up for community development at meetings of the European Social Platform, a forum for non-governmental organisations, which can influence the EU.

Applying the concepts of civil society, social capital and social inclusion will be influenced profoundly by the effects of the EU's enlargement of 2004 from 15 to 25 member states. I am thinking here not of the budgetary implications for the EU, nor of the programmes needed to support the struggle against poverty and social exclusion in most of the new member states, but of the political traditions in Eastern and Central Europe and the importance of civil society. This will change the European context of community development and social exclusion in major ways. Jeremy Rifkin argues that the biggest political change of the past three decades has been the growing involvement of the civil society sector in the political process: "These civil society movements transcend the territorial boundaries of nation states. Their vision is universal.... The European Union has become the place where these movements are beginning to make their voices heard, inside as well as outside the corridors of political power" (Rifkin, 2004, p 241).

THREE

Practice examples and key messages

In the following examples, the two arguments identified by the Combat Poverty Agency for adopting a community development approach to tackling poverty can be seen to be at work:

> The argument for community development, from a social inclusion perspective, is rooted in a broad understanding of citizenship that sees people as having a right to influence and participate in the decisions that affect them and to have their views and experiences listened to and acted on. Community development is potentially a means or process whereby people can achieve this right.

> The second argument is a pragmatic one, which emphasises efficiency and effectiveness. Policies, programmes and services are much more likely to be efficient and effective if those with direct experience of the problems or those who live in communities affected by these problems, are involved in the design and implementation of solutions. (Combat Poverty Agency, 2000, p 5)

The examples illustrate the range and variety of projects set up in communities as responses to social exclusion, as well as the different methods used. The working groups referred to reflect the approach and terminology used in CEBSD's project. The examples from Denmark and Hungary were prepared following the CEBSD project.

Bradford (UK)

Bradford is situated in the North of England and grew at the time of the industrial revolution. In the post-war years, the city remained a focus for immigrants, initially with many displaced people coming from Poland, the Baltic countries and the Balkans and, later, from the countries within the new Commonwealth (particularly Pakistan). It is now one of the most multicultural cities in the UK.

One of the projects studied by the Bradford working group was 'Sharing Voices Bradford', a mental health and community development project. Here a group of staff, committee members and volunteers participate in a day conference discussing the project's future.

It is recognised that the Asian communities experience high levels of poverty and unemployment. However, social exclusion is by no means limited to these communities. On the fringe of the city there are a number of former local authority housing estates that, over the past decade, have experienced high levels of the key indicators of social exclusion: unemployment, low educational achievement, poor health, run-down housing and high levels of crime.

Partly as a reflection of the high levels of social exclusion, there have been a number of major civil disturbances in Bradford over the past 10 years. The largest of these occurred in July 2001 when a proposed National Front march sparked a riot.

There is a long tradition of community development work in Bradford. It has tended to be centre and project based, with an emphasis on neighbourhoods. Recently, community development workers have become increasingly involved in issues of increased participation of local people in planning and decision making around public services. This change of emphasis has also led to a renewed focus on communities of interest (for example Black and minority ethnic communities, gay and lesbian communities, disability communities), in addition to working with well-established neighbourhood-based communities. The existence of a structure for community development in Bradford (currently being reviewed by the local authority) has provided an important basis for the following practice examples explored by the Bradford working group.

The café in the park. This was a youth-led campaign. A young person had died and, to commemorate his memory, a group of young people wished to set up a café in the park where they had always met together. It was their dream, not an identified need. They raised the funding to do it, but then failed to get planning permission from the authorities. They were offered another location but this did not have the same meaning to them. As a result they returned the funding and gave up their plans.

From dying church to new community centre. A church with a dwindling congregation was altered and extended to create a new community centre. Initially there was tension between the former church attendees and representatives of the local community but this was handled effectively by the community development worker. The example highlights how, in some circumstances, it is beneficial to have former professionals (teachers, social workers) from outside the area involved in the management of a project. This challenges the idea that all community initiatives need to be locally managed at all stages.

Sharing Voices Bradford. This is a mental health project that uses community development principles and methods. It was set up, with funding for three years from the Primary Care Trust for central Bradford, because of growing evidence that Black and minority ethnic communities were not using the statutory mental health services. The project seeks to challenge the medical model of mental health, to demystify psychiatry and to promote people with mental health problems themselves as the experts. The project is working with a wide range of self-help and community groups and it is using a group of 10 volunteers to help extend the work. Its funding has been extended for a further two years.

Hutson Street Café. This is an example of using people's interest in food to unite different communities. A community group runs the café. It offers a world cuisine from a building located in one of the demolition areas near the centre of the city. The idea of the café stemmed from the dream of local residents, received funding and is now hoping to move towards becoming a community enterprise. In addition to offering healthy food, it provides opportunities for volunteers and job training.

The experience of a community activist. Without effective support, activists and volunteers can run out of steam and become disillusioned. One person's experience is described in this example. She was heavily involved in community action and then studied for a degree in community development with the aim of becoming a paid community development worker.

Neighbourhood Support Service. This example draws attention to the role that a local authority can play in increasing local participation. It looked, in particular, at neighbourhood forums and the promotion of partnerships. Forums can provide access to information, politicians and local government officers. They can also be a way of having two-way consultation, of building relationships and networks and of playing a role in conflict mediation between and within communities. Two examples of partnerships were discussed. The Frizinghall Partnership initially involved a 'top-down' approach. This was appropriate as the community was too disengaged at the outset of the initiative to launch it 'bottom up'. Local residents are now getting involved. The Shipley Community Arts Network is less formal and looser in its structure. However, it has played a major role in attracting support for a community arts approach to community development. Words can attract involvement but evidence of action sustains it.

Learning from community development practice

Developments in communities are ongoing. Community development often involves a cyclical process whereby initiatives are born, develop, flourish or not, and then die down in response to social, environmental and economic needs. Other key points identified by the working group were:

- Communities are fluid, dynamic and evolving, not fixed and static.
- Methods for evaluating community development need to incorporate this point. They also need to focus on both quantitative and qualitative material. Communities need to be involved in designing and following through the evaluation process.
- Priorities and agendas within communities will shift in response to local and international events, for example riots or September 11. This will impact on local community development initiatives. The strength of community development workers is their closeness to communities. They can gain the trust and confidence of local people. They are not seen as an authority, or as holding power over individuals or groups. Through facilitation and working with the priorities of local people, they have the capacity to address power imbalances. In this way, they can enable communities to share in the process of 'setting the agenda'.

Sharing Voices Bradford: A group of staff, volunteers and children celebrate a festival in the project's building.

- The case studies of community development in Bradford reflect the variety of approaches that are necessary if progress is to be made. By taking a holistic view when responding to needs, compartmentalised thinking can be avoided and the joined-up thinking required to tackle societal issues can develop.
- Community development workers increasingly see the importance of meeting in forums to share information and to learn from each other and from mentors.
- Interagency and partnership work can be very effective when organised and resourced and can involve local authority workers playing a key role in engaging in the community development process.

Holmlia Community Foundation (Norway)

Holmlia is in a part of Oslo called Søndre Nordstrand, one of the city's biggest and newest residential areas. The area consists of 4,500 flats and has 12,000 inhabitants. The flats are divided into 25 housing cooperatives. There is a high proportion of children and young people among the population and the birth rate indicates that the area will continue to have a 'young' population. One in four inhabitants are immigrants from non-Western countries. The people in the area represent 54 different nations and 124 languages are spoken. During a four-year period (1981-85) 11,000 people moved into this area.

What was common to a lot of them was that they did not have a local network. They did not know the surroundings that they had moved into. This resulted in many of them feeling insecure. They did not have a sense of belonging and this resulted in a lack of responsibility. Holmlia received negative coverage in the media and this reinforced feelings of insecurity. At the end of the 1980s, a project was initiated to increase residents' well-being and feelings of safety. When the project finished, four of the cooperatives and the original project joined forces to create the Holmlia Community Foundation (HCF).

The project focuses on the following issues:

* making connections and networking;
* environmental action;
* a community newspaper;
* creating a positive image of Holmlia;
* making public services aware of residents' needs.

Specific projects are:

The Night Ravens. This is a group of adults volunteering to take nightly walks in the area at evening and night time. They meet every Friday and some Saturdays to prevent disturbances and crime among the young people in the area. The Night Ravens have been in operation since 1992. They cooperate closely with the community security guard and the youth team.

Community security guard. A local security guard works under HCF and patrols the area at night time. Irregularities are reported immediately to the head of the Board at the housing cooperative, and the manager of HCF provides monthly reports. This means that contact is quick and problems can be resolved. Again, there is a close cooperation between HCF, the community security guard, the child welfare team, the police, youth club leaders and the Night Ravens.

Environmental patrol. This consists of children, young people and adults who work to clean up the communal areas and, through these activities, prevent the dropping of litter and vandalism. Working together makes the patrol more aware of the effect of their actions. It has existed since 1991 and has become a model for similar projects in other parts of Oslo and in Sarajevo.

Community newspaper. The paper has become a very useful channel of information for voluntary organisations, the local administration, schools and residents. It is led by an editorial group, which consists of volunteers and the manager of HCF who is also the editor. It comes out four times a year and is distributed to everyone living in Holmlia.

Annual meetings and conferences. Meetings with different themes, conferences, seminars and so on are organised for residents. This helps communication and contact and strengthens social networks in the community. Once a year the residents, representatives from the housing cooperatives, employers from the administration and other cooperation partners meet to exchange visions for the community and plan new activities. There is also a friendship group for elderly people of different ethnic backgrounds, a film club and an arts club especially for children.

What has been learned is that:

- To achieve real community participation, there has to be a shared agreement that it is important to deal with a problem or challenge.
- It is necessary to work actively to bring together community resources.
- Plans have to be adjusted to the local situation. Spontaneity has to be part of the approach, responding to what 'comes up' in a neighbourhood.
- There has to be room for non-traditional forms of cooperation, especially when tasks are to be undertaken by a partnership between the local council and the community. The aim is to create dialogue in venues where local people have a sense of belonging.
- There has to be reciprocal and clear communication at all levels. Access to information is crucial and sharing information face to face by door knocking can be a good supplement to written information. Using pictures and symbols is also important.
- Above all, people's lives are not divided into different sections. Services need to have a holistic approach, making the effort always to see the whole person.
- HCF's main goal has been to create a safe, inclusive and attractive community, to strengthen the sense of identity, to coordinate forces and work towards communal solutions for the individual, organisations and public bodies.

It has been difficult to maintain the focus on the most vulnerable groups, partly because HCF has been wary of stigmatising them further. However, over a period of 12 years, a lot of experiences, methods and tools have been created in relation to inclusiveness, participation and prevention. This represents a good reply to the search by the Ministry of Social Affairs for best practice in relation to the goal of creating an inclusive society (expressed in the Norwegian National Action Plan, White Paper no 6 [2002-03], *Action plan against poverty*).

The working group that studied Holmlia continued to meet after CEBSD's project had finished.

Ghent (Belgium)

Until the 1970s, New Ghent (Nieuw Gent) was still a rural, agricultural area. This altered drastically when three housing associations began to build social housing there. In a short time, the area became home to some 6,000 'Nieuw Gentenaars'.

At the outset, the intention was to provide accommodation principally for students and commuters working in the city. Over the years, the target group became increasingly restricted to the most vulnerable groups. Now the tower blocks house mainly single people, those people on social benefit and non-nationals (70 different nationalities!).

It was in such a setting that, in April 2000, a welfare office was opened. This 'open house' was the base for a series of social services: OCMW (Social Welfare Office), Kind en Gezin (Child and the Family), Stedelijk Buurtwerking (Municipal Community Development Work), the Intercultural Network and RISO (Regional Community Development Work). It was also the new home for Wijkresto & Co, a community restaurant run for and by local people. Each year, some 30 or so volunteers help out in this project, backed up by a coordinator and four unemployed people from the area.

Since the project started, the activities have been extended to include Wijkresto & Co, while related projects have been developed to improve living conditions in the area and to promote social cohesion. All the new projects sprang from the ideas of local people and were implemented in partnership with the private sector, municipal services and community organisations. In more concrete terms:

- The bicycle shed project: 83 metal bicycle sheds were made available, free, to people living in the tower blocks.
- The local barbecue project: a site was fitted out with tables and benches, and a fixed barbecue was installed to be used free by individuals and groups.

Wijkresto & Co: The community restaurant's logo on Nieuw Gent.

- Local Olympics: Olympic Games are organised at the local level with sports such as darts, Turkish wrestling and Chinese *tai ji*.

Job design in Wijkresto & Co

The unique aspect of personnel policy in Wijkresto & Co is that paid and unpaid staff work side by side. It is a formula that works wonderfully well. There are more than enough volunteers (other community organisations all too often cannot find any) and the cooperation with the paid workers is excellent (other organisations often see such cooperation as impossible). This led us to reflect on and identify the factors for such success. In our opinion, the answer lies in our attention to job design.

Involvement

One of the basic principles is that everyone is involved in running the project. This far-reaching form of participation means that volunteers, staff, customers and other organisations can make suggestions, take part in decision making and determine organisational policy. The coordinator ensures that the basic conditions are such that everyone's opinion can be heard. Paid staff provide back-up for the volunteers (not vice versa).

Consequence: everyone sees that he or she can influence the way things function, there is open discussion and there is a broad basis for the way things work. People have the feeling that they are taken

Wijkresto & Co: Staff, volunteers and customers enjoy a meal in the restaurant.

seriously and this motivates them to share the responsibility for how things function.

Financial benefits

Everyone derives financial benefit: staff receive a wage (everyone, moreover, receives the same basic wage regardless of the job package – the rate is above the current rates in the hotel and catering sector); volunteers receive an honorarium. At the end of the month, this often makes a difference for them.

Consequence: a little extra for people who, in general, have no more prospects of a higher income due to inability to work or because they are pensioners or people with mental health difficulties.

Training opportunities

Co-workers are appointed on the basis of their needs (*not* on the basis of their abilities). A generous annual training budget is available for both volunteers and staff. For volunteers, training activities are organised on a group basis (for example educational excursions to another community restaurant, taking part in study days, cooking lessons). In addition, staff can follow individual training courses (for example computer training, hygiene, training as assistant cooks).

A social safety net

Co-workers are part of a social network in which much attention is paid to respect and the ability to help. This provides a breathing space and an anchor for people who very often come from a situation of isolation. In addition, everyone can come to the network with any sort of problem. There is also individual support for those who wish it.

Consequence: people feel that there is someone they can approach and, strangely enough, they gain a better grasp of their own position.

Work made to measure with opportunities for self-improvement

Co-workers (paid and unpaid) decide their individual work roster and their jobs. Moreover, the job package is flexible so that co-workers can always take on new challenges and opportunities to learn. Their situations – physical, psychological, family – are also taken very much into account.

Consequence: it is easy to persevere in the work, which gives people a sense of success.

Good practice model

The material in this section was provided by Ann Bonte and Anniek Vandecasteele of the Ghent working group. The group continued to meet after CEBSD's project had finished and it has developed a model of good practice based on its work with local people. The model uses the concept of a house, as described next.

To combat poverty, community work must:

- begin from the grassroots and be democratic – *the basic foundation*;
- contribute to the structural solution of a collective problem – *the walls and the roof*;
- organise ongoing consultation – *the doorstep*;
- be easily accessible – *the kitchen*;
- develop group activities – *the living room*;
- have open communication and make information accessible – *the windows and doors*;
- create opportunities – *comfort*.

For each stage of the model, key words can be identified and specific questions asked. For example, in order to communicate we must first of all *listen*. To exchange knowledge, information must be *understandable and accessible* to a group. A community worker must *provide information* and *stimulate exchange*. The questions would include:

- What information is distributed about the project? To whom? When?
- What kinds of external information are at participants' disposal?
- How do you know if the information is sufficiently comprehensible?
- Is there enough information to be able to refer people?

A simple assessment scale is used against each criterion, helping a group to see in what ways things can be improved. This kind of good practice can be used as an example with other projects. It can also be helpful for making policy choices.

A leaflet explaining the model is available from CEBSD's Belgian member, VIBOSO (see Appendix B for contact details).

Orebro (Sweden)

The Baronbackarna housing estate was built 50 years ago in the west part of Orebro, a city of 114,000 inhabitants. Two thousand people live on the estate, which was one of the first in Sweden to have a long-term perspective on housing policy – not just securing a roof over people's heads but also providing the means for a good life in terms of social conditions and facilities, health and the environment.

However, life today for most people on Baronbackarna does not match up to the ideals of its founders. Living conditions vary considerably, there is social and ethnic segregation and there is inequality between men and women. How this has happened can be seen in the work undertaken for the development of the area, particularly by the establishment of a labour cooperative.

Key data:

- ethnically Swedish: 44.6%
- ethnically foreign: 55.4%
- employed: 48.7% (rest of the council area: 73.2%)
- unemployed: 12.4% (rest of area: 4.4%)
- on social security: 31% (rest of area: 7.3%)
- election turnout 2002: 64% (area average: 80.6%).

There is evidence that social and economic factors are impacting on people's health. The living conditions bring about a feeling of powerlessness rather than self-determination. It was the existence of this situation that led to the setting-up of an employment project.

The Kullen cooperative

A self-empowerment project in Baronbackarna is taking place within the framework of the EU's EQUAL programme, which aims to counteract discrimination and inequality. In the project's list of aims and activities there is a strong commitment to establish a labour cooperative. This became a reality in March 2003 in the Kullen cooperative. The cooperative has become the arena for the creation of self-empowerment and influence on the estate. Key outcomes have been:

* being able to describe the sense of alienation among people from the perspective of those who have first-hand experience of alienation;
* being able to identify factors in the labour market that are discriminatory;
* having a goal for the cooperative to become independent of external support by the end of 2004;
* approximately 130 people have benefited directly from the project over an 18-month period.

The project sets out to make use of the life experiences of each individual. It is committed to broadening the local labour market by, for example, utilising the security of the estate and the proximity between companies and workers. It develops both work and community because it builds on the interests, skills and needs of people.

The cooperative has given a clear message that anyone who, for some reason, is outside the ordinary labour market has the right to work in a social labour cooperative. If, for example, someone has a functional disorder which means he or she has a reduced capacity to work, that person is eligible to participate and the labour exchange will determine the size of the allowance to be allocated to the cooperative. Long-term dependency on social security is another valid reason. Members of the cooperative have been outside the ordinary labour market for between two and 20 years.

The cooperative has become aware of the extent to which public institutions and their regulations fail to take active measures to obtain an individual's transition to employment. There is access to employment, but the institutions cannot link the needs of individuals to public resources. The cooperative has also realised how society as a whole distrusts those people who are outside the traditional labour market. This is central to the discrimination that is experienced.

Considerable progress has been made by the cooperative. It has been accepted as a tenderer and it has started a cleaning and maintenance service company in which five people are already certified cleaners. The company has been successful in winning contracts. The social benefits arising from the existence of the cooperative are clear: if, for example, someone is ill for a long time, he or she can use the cooperative as a starting point or platform for his or her rehabilitation. A cooperative can act as a gateway to a range of solutions for individuals.

There is a saving on the public purse resulting from this kind of support. It also means that the need for longer rehabilitation measures is reduced. However, sustaining a cooperative such as Kullen is often undermined because of the difficulty of obtaining resources to enable members of the cooperative to access education and training. The cooperative's survival is also highly dependent on the commitment and self-reliance of its members. People need to be touched emotionally if they are to get involved and stay involved. "Work with trust and think economically" is the key message from the Orebro group.

Barcelona (Spain)

The Barcelona working group focused on four neighbourhood-based community plans or participation processes. Three of them are described next.

A neighbourhood participation council in Sant Cosme, el Prat del Llobregat. Research was carried out by the local authority in 2000 to assess the feasibility of local participation. As a result of the process, a neighbourhood participation council was set up. It consists of representatives from neighbourhood groups and statutory organisations. The purpose is to share ideas and proposals. There is a coordinating commission (monthly meetings) as well as several working groups.

A community plan in Torre Baro, Barcelona. A process of change was set in motion in 2000 jointly by the neighbourhood association for Torre Baro and the local authority for the Nou Barris district. To begin with the plan was concerned almost entirely with physical changes in the neighbourhood. Soon, however, a wider perspective emerged that embraced community development, health, education and employment. A range of groups and organisations work in partnership.

A community plan in Sant Josep, Reus. Here, too, there is involvement both by community groups and professionals. The plan was based on a participatory appraisal of the neighbourhood – its problems but also its potential. Working groups were set up on 'being neighbours', young people, regeneration, the image of the neighbourhood and drug misuse. Proposals by the groups are brought together to provide an integral vision for the future.

The Barcelona working group thought that the idea of neighbourhood participation originated in the late 1970s. At that time, the mobilisation of neighbourhoods in the new political context of democracy was impressive. However, from the mid-1980s, the social movement dimension of neighbourhood action lost its momentum; the opportunity for neighbourhood action to strengthen the role of civil society was lost. For much of the history of Catalonia, participation had been hidden. It was not easy for people to meet. When democracy came, many social movements turned themselves into political parties.

The current situation is characterised by two developments:

- Local authorities are seeking to put in place a 'relationship model' with community groups. This, however, leads to dependency and does little to tackle the causes of social problems, fragmentation and lack of coordination.
- As a consequence of the weakness of communities in the context of civil society, there is a strong individualism and a lack of social identity in neighbourhoods.

The community development approach puts an emphasis on education and on finding ways of getting politicians to listen to communities. There is no doubt that local people can become 'motors for change' in their neighbourhoods. The community plans are designed to find ways of addressing neighbourhood problems. Research is undertaken on social cohesion, the role of key actors in any one neighbourhood and the scope for changing the way problems are addressed and the need for local councils to provide support. A team approach to undertaking a community plan, in partnership with local people, is adopted. While it is important – to boost confidence – to get results in the short to medium term, it is essential to allow plenty of time for the processes of planning and community organisation to take place. This is often a problem because of the prevalent culture of expecting everything to happen immediately and because politicians tend to think only of the short term. Community development work needs long-term support, not just between elections.

All service providers need to participate in the planning process. There is a lack of interdepartmental cooperation and coordination in the city council. It is also essential to motivate council officers to take a community development approach. Community development workers can be seen as a threat by the authorities. Workers are often employed by neighbourhood associations and their posts are dependent on resources that can take a long time to arrive.

In some areas, progress is slow because of the extent to which local people are dependent on public assistance. This generates a 'receiving' culture and achieving participation is difficult. Also, in some areas, individuals who see themselves as leaders are not always effective. In the opinion of the Barcelona working group, it is important to take an egalitarian approach whereby everyone works at the same level.

The emphasis now is on civic participation. There is a poor relationship between the authorities and local people, and civic participation aims to change this. However, developments are fragmentary and there is a need for greater transparency in decision-making processes and structures. Authorities need to change their policies. They also have to address the needs of different generations. The main purpose of community development is to organise for transformation and, where there are conflicts, to try to mediate.

Copenhagen (Denmark)

Vesterbro is the oldest working-class neighbourhood in Copenhagen, close to the main railway station and near the medieval centre of the city. Entertainment, pubs and prostitution have always been, and still are, big business and since the 1970s drug dealing has been added to that list. In the 1950s, the area was densely populated (approximately 65,000 people). By the mid-1980s, the neighbourhood looked neglected. Unemployment was high because the unskilled jobs in industry had disappeared from the city. Community development was sporadic, lacking any focus or strength. As a response to this situation, the Christian Student Settlement started an initiative called the Sidestreet project. The Settlement is a non-governmental organisation that has worked in Vesterbro for almost 100 years.

Volunteers and children outside the settlement house in Copenhagen.

The focus of the project was twofold: first, there was a need to reopen shops in order to improve everyday life, local social services and the market for people living there; second, there was a need to create meaningful jobs for young working-class people who had little or no education and few job possibilities. The project turned out to be the beginning of a new community development approach, creating new communities among people and at the same time creating jobs and shops.

Urban renewal and gentrification

By 2004, however, Vesterbro had become 'gentrified'. The area has been improved through a large urban renewal programme, many flats have become bigger (by turning two flats into one) and much more expensive. The population is now approximately 35,000. The former working-class area with a culture bound together by common experiences is now a population with big differences in income and living standards, ethnic and cultural backgrounds, health and education. Young middle-income families with children are dominating the area, dividing – or bridging? – the gap with the 20% of the population who are, to a greater or lesser extent, socially excluded because of mental or physical illness, heavy stress, abuse problems, or lack of money, housing, a job or education.

New role for local voluntary organisations

These changes meant that the Settlement had to adjust: the Sidestreet project had shown how to respond to new needs; now the old organisation had to find new ways to make the transition from being a traditional institution into a modern community development organisation.

Over the last five years, the Settlement has focused on developing new types of community development projects. Central to them is the ability to combine a bottom–up approach, that is the empowerment of grassroots and users, with stronger networking and cooperation with mainstream bodies such as statutory organisations. The achievement has been to improve the possibilities for people to network and meet across the borders of cultural and social connections and communities. Networking in this context is seen as a means to enabling people to cope with an increasingly individualised and multicultural community.

Network, Talk and Sport – on Prescription!

One of the projects has focused on combining the need of individuals to have the opportunity for social and psychological consultation and support with offers of joining local sports and exercising activities as well as networking activities. The name of the project is Network, Talk and Sport – on Prescription!

Target groups for the project are people who feel isolated and who are trapped in their lives. They may have lifestyle problems (weight problems, abuse problems and so on). Many seek treatment from their local doctor. The project has established an unusual partnership with the local health board – that is, the doctors, health visitors and district nurses. These professionals, who meet people with special needs at a consultation or in their homes, can give a prescription for three alternative treatments:

1. an exercise activity in one of the local sports clubs and free membership for six months. New classes are set up with a special focus on, for example, elderly people, Muslim women or young people with interests in yoga and so on;
2. a number of free sessions with a psychologist or therapist;
3. a networking activity with other people.

The doctors can prescribe all the three offers or just one or two, depending on the wishes and needs of each person. This prescription can be an alternative to anti-depressive medicine or can be given as a supplement.

The doctors have been very positive about the project. In the first six months, about one third of them used the new form of prescription. At a seminar held by the project, one doctor said: "Because we know how dangerous it is to be socially isolated, children should learn about this project in school!".

In the first six months, about 60 people chose to use the prescription and to start two or all three activities. The profile of the users shows a very differentiated picture – a mirror of the population of Vesterbro – as shown in the following examples.

A male refugee from Iran, who has a Master's degree in social science and who speaks seven languages, gets a prescription to the project from his doctor. He would like to start exercising with a sports association and get into a social network. He had been imprisoned in Iran for 14 years and is traumatised. He lives alone, cannot get employment and spends his days reading. In the morning, he goes to the library to borrow a book, which he then returns in the evening. He describes his life as free but completely empty. The networker introduces him to a trainer and he starts exercising in one of the small teams. Parallel to this, the networker meets with him once a week to talk about what kind of network and activity he would like to join. They find two activities: he would like to become a volunteer driver and he wants to become a member of a lunch club.

A single mother of two children contacts the project after receiving a prescription from her health visitor. She has lived all her life in the same neighbourhood. Since the local brewery, where she had worked, closed down 10 years ago she has not had a job. Last year, she went back to school in order to get an education, being the first in her family to do so. Now, however, she is on the verge of abandoning this. She has been ill for the last two months, being very overweight and feeling incapable and lonely as both a student and a mother. She would like to have sessions with the therapist and to find a family activity where she can meet other parents and where her children can play with other children.

Network, Talk and Sport not a hit – yet

The 'hits' of the project have been the prescription for sports activities and the individual sessions with a therapist. The networking activities have received far fewer users. For the time being, we do not know the reasons for this. Perhaps the purpose of the networking activities is not as clear as the talk sessions and the sports activities. The networking activities need to be organised in new and sensitive ways in dialogue with the users and volunteers.

By acknowledging the basic conditions necessary for this work, we believe it is possible to improve access to social networks – and these basic conditions are:

- meaningful activities in a local context;
- time and patience;
- the provision of support to help people form good interpersonal relationships.

In that way, each of the three types of prescription can inform and influence each other.

Upper Kiskunsag and Dunamellek (Hungary)

Upper Kiskunsag and Dunamellek is one of the most disadvantaged regions of Hungary. It is only 50 miles south of Budapest but experiences a range of rural problems. The area covers 500 square miles. The population is 32,000 and there are 10 villages.

Community development work was undertaken in five communities, a town and four villages. Kunbabony is a hamlet with 300 inhabitants. It belongs to the town of Kunszentmiklos and does not have its own council or school. Development work started in Kunbabony because the Civil College, the training centre of the Hungarian Association for Community Development, is situated there.

The results of initial contact-making and information-gathering confirmed the extent of the problems being experienced by the community:

- unemployment, lack of economic potential, poor education;
- weak infrastructure and institutions;
- low land value and agricultural experience resulting from earlier state cooperatives and big farms;

- lack of a sense of community with very few voluntary or community organisations;
- isolation of young people;
- paternalistic style of the local authorities: no awareness of the concept of development and no leaders to take initiatives.

Stages of the community development process

1. 1997-98. Getting to know each other, identifying problems, involving local people:

- The community workers visit organisations, especially the local authorities, to introduce themselves. They also arrange meetings in the Civil College to discuss the region and some possible objectives.
- Interviews with about 200 families in the five communities are planned and carried out. They involve students as well as the community workers.
- Discussions are held in each local community.

2. 1998-99. Training community workers:

- Exploratory work: finding local people who would welcome change in their community and who would be willing to take an initiative.
- One year of training for community leaders (one weekend each month), as well as working meetings.
- Fieldwork: with the participants on the training course, the launch of local development processes. In Kunbabony, for example, this consisted of organising cultural and community events, helping elderly people and those in need by providing seeds and giving advice on how to produce plants for home use, launching and running a local newspaper, setting up bus stops, creating a playground and ensuring improved refuse collection. Similar activities were encouraged in the other villages.

3. 1999. Formalisation and institutionalisation:

- Planning the organisation of community workers in Upper Kiskunsag, including the setting up of an association.
- Fundraising for jobs for the participants on the training course. To date, two people have been employed by the regional association.

4. 2000-03. Regional economic development programme:

This stage of the process had been preceded by a cooperative development programme and a training programme in the secondary school for developing a culture favourable to economic development. There had also been a mentoring programme to support unemployed people.

- Involvement of key representatives of local government and the voluntary and business sectors.
- A regional economic planning workshop (run four times).
- Setting up an information centre in each village and providing training for the leaders of the centres.
- Establishing a regional economic development foundation.
- Organising a regional economic exhibition and starting a regional newspaper.
- Launching local job creation schemes (employing Roma, building a greenhouse, raising seedlings, improving the town's image, running a community centre, an Internet café and a telecommunications centre).

5. Reviewing the regional work:

- Preparation of a three-year strategic plan with the community workers' association. Future activities to include training for community workers, strengthening the network and partnerships and formalising cooperation among voluntary organisations.
- These developments are unprecedented in Hungarian community development and represent important models. Community workers tend to work on their own, and having a professional support network has been invaluable. The workers have supported each other through visits, discussions and training.
- Identifying and encouraging local community leaders has been a major difficulty. One reason for this is the strength of family and friendship ties in the local communities. In addition, there is an expectation that local government will make all the decisions about communities – there is no tradition of participation. Those in power are unwilling to share decisions and responsibilities.
- Encouraging small farmers and others to work cooperatively has been a major challenge, especially because of the low level of technological knowledge and marketing skills. Training for enterprise and business, therefore, needed to be a priority. The first

cooperative began functioning in 1999 with 15 members. It had been preceded by many discussions with individuals and at public meetings. The cooperative does not have paid management but it can provide a minimal level of organisation. As a result of the development process in Kunbabony, a regional pig farming cooperative has been established.

Funding for the community development work has come from the Hungarian Association for Community Development, which raised money from sources outside Hungary. So far, there has been no support from the region. The regional and local associations have been able to raise funds for specific local projects but not for the development work.

Not having to meet performance expectations or obligations has meant that the work in Upper Kiskunsag has been sustained by professional commitment. This has brought visible results. So far, however, the local authorities in the region, while they acknowledge what has been achieved, have failed to recognise the value of the work by supporting it.

Key messages

Imagine a small discussion group consisting of experienced community workers and members of community groups. They have listened to the examples summarised earlier in this chapter. Indeed, some of them took part in the actions. Now they decide to specify the practice lessons that can be drawn from the examples as a whole: an overall analysis. The lessons are not abstract principles, nor are they theoretical statements. Rather they are practical points that members of the group, as people who are experienced in community development and social inclusion work, think should be given close consideration in order for effective practice to be achieved. These are the key messages that they identified – not in any order, and organised under four headings.

Involvement

- People are motivated more by dreams than needs. It is important to focus on what people want to see happen rather than what is established as a 'need'.
- Community workers need to consider what the barriers are to participation, thinking especially of the needs of activists and volunteers, for example childcare.

- Community workers have a role in ensuring that equality issues are addressed and that community projects are inclusive.
- Test out ideas first, see if they will win support among local people.
- The focus on groups should not obscure the importance of individuals, who often need lots of support. Time spent doing this is often not tangible.
- Try to have social and inclusive meeting places that encourage a sense of belonging, respect and dialogue with decision makers.
- Always try to use an inclusive, common language – no jargon.
- Equally, information on what is happening in a neighbourhood or the local authority should be inclusive. A variety of methods should be used. Not everybody has access to the Internet and a personal computer.
- People will expect to see changes if they are to continue their involvement.

Organisation

- Ensuring that development takes place at a pace that is appropriate for the community is vital. There are considerable advantages when community development makes a long-term commitment, as can be seen in the Hungarian example.
- Community workers and community groups need to face outwards as well as inwards: engagement and partnerships with local institutions and service providers as well as building the resources of a group. The Bradford and Copenhagen examples illustrate this point.
- Be ready to help groups move from working on one issue to another. Note the range of issues illustrated in the seven case studies.
- Having clear objectives is essential in community development. The objectives can change, and they can be reached by being flexible, but if the objectives are not clear it is likely that things will go wrong. Community development has to be strategic.
- The aim should be to help groups become self-reliant and autonomous. Often, however, it is essential that funding is sustained.
- Often community workers will need to combine working with communities of interest and neighbourhood groups.
- Find ways of responding to communities' concerns or fears about control (for example young people). Community workers should not romanticise communities. The Norwegian example of the Night Ravens illustrates this point.

- You cannot have participation without doing something concrete.
- Always seek to work with others and to reduce competition between groups.
- Resistance can create commitment and initiatives from which lessons can be learned. In conflict situations, there is energy that can be liberated in positive directions.

Innovation

- There is a need to have an eye for opportunities, to be reactive and to use innovative methods: lateral thinking, not on tramlines. The example from Bradford of the church turned into a community centre makes the point: the initial group was made up of people from outside the area, not within it.
- Be ready to try out different ways of holding meetings – based on dialogue.

Learning

- There is a need to increase understanding of local people about each other by bringing people from different backgrounds together.
- By building trust between members of a group, the community worker can encourage self-confidence in people, increasing their awareness of how much they have to contribute to strengthening the community.
- Recognise the competence that results from the experiences of community groups.
- Good community development initiatives deliver possibilities for learning to both individuals and groups.
- Reflection needs to be part of the community development process so that participants can make connections between the process and the outcomes.
- Training that is accessed through community development should consider the needs of groups in terms of approach and methods as well as content.
- Networking is an important way of getting communities to see how things are in other communities.

The key messages set out here provide indications of good practice. They can form the basis of sharing and discussion, and they can be built on. The working group in Oslo did this. It has continued to meet and reflect on the outcomes of the European project for work being done in Norway. It produced a way of demonstrating the connections between the basis of good practice for social inclusion work, the paramount and subordinate principles and the indicators of social inclusion (see Table 3.1). It gives an insight into the thinking and priorities of one of the working groups involved in CEBSD's European project. I am grateful to Elisabeth Ostrem for preparing the framework in Table 3.1.

Exploring key messages deriving from good practice leads us to raise the question: What are the principles on which good practice in community development and social exclusion work should be based? The question is important because those people and organisations involved in community development responses to social exclusion need to have a basis on which to make decisions about practice. We shall see that shared principles are not remote from practice. Quite the reverse, we shall argue that they provide an essential foundation for practice.

Table 3.1: Good practice in social inclusion work

Basis of good practice for social inclusion work	Paramount principles of social inclusion	Subordinate principles of social inclusion	Indicators of social inclusion
Political interest in local development	Accessibility	Meeting places	Geographical proximity
			Affordability
			Openness to all groups
Community groups are not charged for the use of public buildings, such as schools		Information	Clear information in language that is easily understandable to all participants (no jargon)
			Comprehensive information: • face to face • Internet/e-mail • meetings using creative methods • posters and so on
Public plans encourage community meetings			Procedures for information and the right to appeal
Investment in and valuing of voluntary work		User-friendliness	Meeting a single professional – 'one-stop' shops
			Rapid response
Stability of measures, such as financial stability	Personal benefit in tangible terms	Benefit individually: for example better standard of living/financial situation	Improved individual situation (work, accommodation, leisure)
Holistic approach to people's needs		Benefit collectively: for example new bus services, playgrounds, better collective facilities	Improved collective situation
Local Agenda 21 work that is less focused on economic growth and more on human development		Acquiring new skills	Increased knowledge and empowerment: • various courses • knowledge required to achieve own goals • knowledge required to achieve collective goals

contd.../

Table 3.1: contd.../

Basis of good practice for social inclusion work	Paramount principles of social inclusion	Subordinate principles of social inclusion	Indicators of social inclusion
Commitment to continuous improvement of services, in partnership with local people	Personal benefit in emotional terms	Experiencing identity	Experiencing relevance of the following statements within the group: • I am important to this group • This group is important for my identity
An understanding of the importance of individuals and organisations cooperating with the public sector	Solidarity	Experiencing being part of a community	Experiencing the relevance of the following statements or principles within the group: • community, equality • My efforts are valued
		Experiencing independence, self-confidence Experiencing joy and dream fulfilment	Experiencing the relevance of the following statements or principles within the group: • I feel independent • I am self-confident • fun activities • room for creativity and exploring art • innovative organisation and methods
A housing policy governed by social needs		Accepting differences	• We are all different • Being different is a good thing • I am accepted the way I am
A focus on deprivation and the excluded		Everybody to have the same rights	Everyone should have the same access to collective goods and help
Education and training opportunities for community development workers		Partnership makes for strength and access to resources	More can be achieved through cooperation than by individuals acting on their own
			When several people experience the same needs, the needs become more visible
	Empowerment/ participation	Proximity to decision making	All involved groups to be heard in ways acceptable to them
			Decisions to be made on the basis of this
Evaluating the results of community development		Genuine authority	The experience of being able to change things
			The experience that it is worth using one's voice/vote

FOUR

Shared principles

The aim of this publication is to identify key points about practice, principles and policy on community development and social exclusion that are shared within the European context. It would, however, be surprising, even strange, if there was always agreement. That would suggest superficiality. Not only are the situations very different across Europe but they also represent different and sometimes contrasting approaches to community development. Thus, while we are looking for what is held in common with regard to principles, we are also alert to differences that reflect the unique political, social and cultural experiences of communities across Europe. We will indicate where there are differences in the following discussion of principles.

Equally important is the need to avoid presenting community development as a panacea. The commitment to be found among those people involved in community development, as well as its idealistic, principled language, make it vulnerable to this tendency. Our concern is to examine the particular contribution of community development to tackling social exclusion. Community development, however, is only one of a number of interventions and methods that are required to make an impact on social exclusion. This point is made by two researchers who refer to the 'fishing trips problem', the fact that many of the activities of community groups are small-scale and appear to have little chance of supporting the more ambitious claims of community development: "small community groups cannot, by themselves, combat the effects of exclusionary forces like poverty, polarization and depopulation. A fishing trip is just a fishing trip" (Richardson and Mumford, 2002, p 225). The researchers, however, do set out ways whereby community groups can contribute to tackling such forces, concluding that:

- Even where problems are too big for community action to tackle alone, community support can help protect other investments (by local and central government for example). Indeed, without it, these investments may be wasted.
- Service-providers, especially in deprived neighbourhoods, should recognise that residents can help them provide stronger

management of neighbourhoods and should enforce controls on behaviour open to them.
- Volunteers and community representatives should be recognised and supported.
- We need to develop new and better ways of measuring the impacts of community activity. (Richardson and Mumford, 2002, p 225)

The researchers usefully depict the multiple benefits of community groups (Figure 4.1).

In setting out the following principles, we do not wish to suggest that they stand separately from each other. On the contrary, it is essential that each principle informs, and is informed by, the other principles; also that good practice is rooted in particular contexts. As one of the working groups in the CEBSD project commented: "What is right in

Figure 4.1: The multiple benefits of community groups

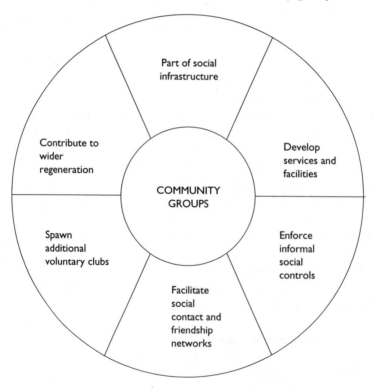

Source: Richardson and Mumford (2002, p 220); reproduced by kind permission of Oxford University Press

Figure 4.2: Principles, practice and action

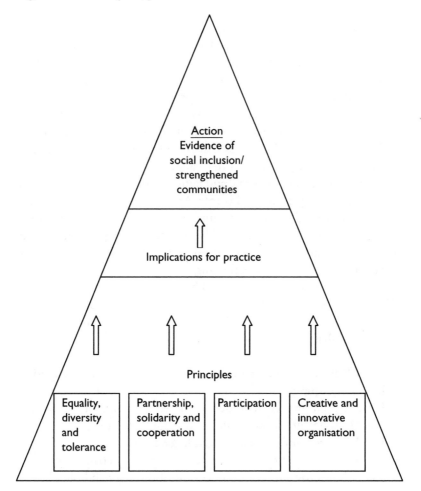

one place can be completely wrong in another." Figure 4.2 shows how the principles connect with practice and action, which in turn lead to stronger communities. For each principle, we suggest what it means in practice. In a final section of the chapter, we address the challenging question of how changes in communities brought about by community development can be measured.

Equality, diversity and tolerance

Working for a fair and just community is at the core of community development. It comes down to how fairly and justly poor, disadvantaged people are treated, not only with regard to the major issues that affect their lives such as housing and employment but also in terms of how people relate to each other. It is for this reason that the principle of equality is inseparable from that of diversity: valuing the variety of cultures, races and faiths. Implied within the principle of equality and diversity is tolerance: being prepared to understand differences as to how people live their lives and, in most instances, being willing to accept the differences. Where this proves to be impossible, then ways need to be found of resolving conflicts and negotiating how people in one neighbourhood can live alongside each other. It is in the latter area that skilled community development workers can often play a key role – alongside other professionals. In some areas, the extent of ethnic and faith divides means that increasing reliance is being placed on this role. As was noted in relation to the intercultural mediation work undertaken by Desenvolupament Comunitari, important links are being made between community development and conflict mediation and resolution. There remains considerable scope for strengthening the connections of community development with peace studies. The Combat Poverty Agency and other organisations in Ireland are bringing together important material based on the EU Peace and Reconciliation Programme. It uses a framework that specifies levels of reconciliation work:

- Level 1: the creation of basic contact, awareness and understanding between groups;
- Level 2: joint projects that involve shared activity, probably around a single issue, but do not address core conflict issues;
- Level 3: core conflict issues are addressed;
- Level 4: joint activity is undertaken, designed to change structures and cultures towards accommodation of diversity and pluralism.

The connections of this approach to peace and reconciliation with community development are evident – the emphasis given to the process of awareness–raising and change.

The main practice implications of the first principle for community development and social exclusion are:

- encouraging more knowledge of different cultural histories;
- communicating knowledge of social systems in different countries;
- increasing understanding of what differences between people and groups mean in particular contexts;
- more appreciation of differences in values and quality of life issues;

- developing clear criteria that can measure commitment to equality, diversity and tolerance in practice;
- supporting a holistic perspective, one that takes account of differences of age, gender, ethnicity, faith and culture and also allows for a focus on specific needs, for example women who are abused.

Partnership, solidarity and cooperation

The word 'partnership' has become so much part of the vocabulary of government regeneration and renewal programmes that its inherent meaning for communities is often in danger of becoming lost. In the context of community development, the idea of partnership is focused above all on the need for groups and networks to work together rather than in isolation from each other or in conflict. The principle of partnership, accordingly, applies primarily to the grassroots level. It connects seamlessly with the notions of solidarity, cooperation and community cohesion: seeking to bring people together and to work cooperatively. Because the demands made of local people who become involved in local activities and action are so considerable, the need to maximise the extent to which people and groups work together has become increasingly evident. The time and energies available for community development are finite. Hence the importance of partnership, solidarity and cooperation at community level.

The application of the principle to relations between communities and statutory organisations is, of course, important too. The need for statutory and other organisations, when they take initiatives, to work in partnership with communities is generally accepted. The key questions turn on how the partnerships are set up and what measures are taken to ensure that the representatives of communities on partnership boards are resourced properly. There is a considerable research literature that indicates that these questions are usually not addressed satisfactorily:

> Partnerships are no more homogeneous than communities, and like communities they are dynamic rather than static, characterised by flux and change. This means that community development support needs to be made available on a continuing, flexible, and long-term basis, rather than in short-term 'special initiatives,' together with access to independent technical advice and training. While this would not of itself guarantee greater equality within partnerships, of course, it could at least begin to redress

> some of the current patterns of inequality and effective
> exclusion. (Mayo and Taylor, 2001, p 53)

It is important that community workers and local leaders do not give up on trying to improve the situation of community groups' representation on partnership boards and on the benefits that partnerships can bring to communities. Partnerships can control significant resources. It is crucial for communities to be represented at decision-making meetings and to debate issues with members of partnership boards. In November 2004, for example, I participated in the annual conference of Wexford Area Partnership in Ireland. The title of the conference was People, Communities and Power. More than 100 participants, including young people and people with learning disabilities, were present and the majority of the participants came from community groups and voluntary organisations. Exchanges of views and the sharing of experiences were lively and the board members will have absorbed some key points. It is possible for partnerships to operate in ways and at a level that maximise the opportunities for communities to be involved in consultation and decision making – we can see this potential in the example of Bradford's Neighbourhood Support Service described in Chapter Three. Partnerships, in short, do not have to be equated with remoteness from communities or decision making behind closed doors.

The importance of partnerships between the statutory, voluntary and private sectors opens up the wider question of the role of local government in community development. This is because, first, it is frequently the local authority that takes the lead role in a partnership and, second, because in many countries local authorities themselves are seeking to engage in more meaningful ways with communities. The case study from Barcelona in Chapter Three reflects this approach: the planning by local authorities for neighbourhoods should be inseparable from community participation.

The phrase 'civic participation' is used in the Barcelona case study to refer to the need to reform local government in ways that will improve its links with communities. The concept of civic society lacks the theoretical and political basis that is integral to the concept of civil society but the significance of the former should not be underestimated. An EU-funded project on citizen participation in local government undertaken under the auspices of Demos, a UK 'think tank', was responding to common concerns in seven countries about citizen apathy and mistrust of government. However, it also drew attention to positive opportunities that exist to revitalise local democracy. The first of a number of guidelines in the report of the project states:

> Governance is about partnership – To achieve good governance, local government must work in equal partnership with representatives from business, community and voluntary groups and civil society such as churches and trade unions. This will only work if local government is prepared to share power with other partners. The challenge of creating an open, trusting atmosphere should not be underestimated – it takes time and hard work. Local government faces a particular challenge to both lead, a key role, and yet accept the views of partners in an egalitarian framework in which each partner feels they have an equal role. (Demos Project, 2004, p 4)

The experience of CEBSD's member organisations is that the willingness and capacity of local government to open up the community development agenda is very uneven within EU member states. There are examples of good practice by local authorities and it is these that community development organisations should take note of and help disseminate. This point was emphasised by Stewart Murdoch, using the example of Dundee in Scotland, in the paper he gave to the workshop on community development and urban regeneration at the 2004 Budapest conference on building civil society in Europe through community development:

> Over the last decade the emphasis placed on partnerships, community involvement and tackling inequalities has started to change the relationship between citizens and the 'local state'.... We still have some way to go, however, if this city is to become a network of healthy, thriving, self-sufficient communities where people choose to live because of the quality of life.

> In all of its recent community development and urban regeneration practice, there has been a concerted effort made in Dundee to reconcile the tensions between the role of local government, the local elected member, community involvement and the creation of a vibrant city where every citizen's contribution to community life and community learning is valued. (Murdoch, 2005: forthcoming)

Accessibility to local authorities and the development of better services are crucially important to deprived communities. This is something that some communities have had to learn: closing off communication with the local authority is, in the end, not an option for any community group, however difficult it may be to establish meaningful dialogue.

The practice implications of the principle of partnership, solidarity and cooperation are:

- The principle needs to be applied at all levels: neighbourhood, local, regional, national/federal, European.
- Cooperation should include professionals, politicians, the private sector and community and non-governmental organisations.

Participation

The principle of participation permeates community development very powerfully at all levels. In community groups and networks, it contains a strong message of a commitment to open membership and the maximum transparency of decision-making processes. Cliques of people who seek to control a group are not acceptable. A good community development worker will make a point of helping groups to have involvement and membership from all parts of a community. This is clearly important when community development is seeking to address the problem of social exclusion: almost by definition, people who are experiencing social exclusion are likely to experience difficulties in joining a community group. It is well known that marginalised people are frequently criticised or ostracised by neighbours. The principle of participation in community development is there to challenge such attitudes. It is also there to demonstrate to decision makers the capabilities of communities. Participation in community affairs can challenge the negative stereotypes that outsiders may hold of communities and set in motion a positive cycle.

Participation – Why Bother?

Participation – Why Bother? was a series of four workshops run by Sharing Voices Bradford and the International Centre for Participation Studies at Bradford University, UK. The events focused on the experiences of participation of Black and minority ethnic communities within the health service, in particular mental health services. The workshops were run informally and a careful record was kept of points made. The focus was on finding out about the experiences people had of participating in public life (being a school governor, a volunteer, an active member of a mosque and so on) – what they could offer – and of identifying the barriers to their participation in the health service. The outcomes of the events were written up and a report was presented to health professionals. Representatives from the four workshops then met with the professionals and put across key messages about how participation levels of Black and minority ethnic communities could be improved. Better information systems and a commitment to greater understanding of particular cultures were identified as priorities. The health service undertook to act on the recommendations.

There will always be contrasting degrees of participation in a community (Figure 4.3). Often a community development worker will be supporting a relatively small but committed group of people. It is important for the worker to remind this group that it is working on behalf of both those people who will benefit directly from a project or initiative (users of community benefits in Figure 4.3) and a wider constituency of people: members of the core group are not there as direct representatives of other people but they should be acting on behalf of other people.

Figure 4.3: Degrees of involvement in community groups

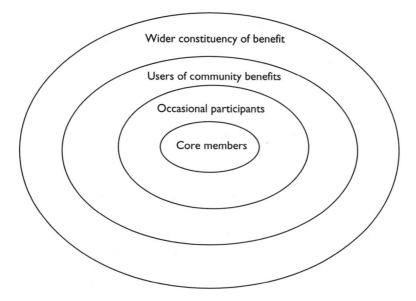

Source: Acknowledgement to H. Salmon

Participation is inherently problematic in community development because there are different degrees of participation. It is so easy, so quick for it to become tokenistic. This is especially likely in the relations between communities and public bodies. Promises are made that communities will be encouraged to participate and then, too often, all that happens is superficial consultation. The Commission on Poverty, Participation and Power in the UK found that, while many people living in poverty were keen to be involved, "years of being ignored or sidelined, or experience of phoney participation, have also left many angry and disillusioned. Again, it will require painstaking and long-term community development work, together with a commitment to genuine involvement, to win over the sceptical and disillusioned" (Lister, 2001, pp viii–ix).

Thus the principle of participation, while being so much part of community development, is profoundly challenging. It applies to many different aspects of community development. We have highlighted the issues of how community groups function and the ways in which public bodies relate to communities, but it is also highly relevant to research (participatory appraisal), governance (how elected bodies relate to a wider constituency) and management (how staff of an organisation can be involved in decision making).

The implications for practice are considerable. Here we would highlight the need for participation to be based on:

- communication and information, flexibility and exchange;
- a commitment to follow-up and to provide feedback;
- the provision of genuine choices;
- transparency and openness;
- accessible services.

Creative and innovative organisation

For many readers, the principle of creative and innovative organisation will be the most surprising of the four principles. There is a twofold explanation as to why it is so important in community development:

- There is a need for community development to work to the traditions and expectations of communities – the ways in which they are prepared to become involved. The point was summarised by Saul Alinsky, the American community organiser, when insisting on the need to stay within the experiences of people you are helping to organise: "The basic requirement for the understanding of the politics of change is to recognise the world as it is. We must work with it on its terms if we are to change it to the kind of world we would like it to be" (Alinsky, 1972, p 12). This means that it will often be necessary to organise in creative and innovative ways, for example: planning meetings that combine task-focused activities and social interaction, respecting cultural and religious procedures for opening and ending meetings, suggesting that people operate as a network rather than necessarily forming themselves into a community group.

- It is important to counter the sense of inferiority or submissiveness that local people can feel when they are confronted with the procedures of formal organisations, for example: meetings controlled by the chairperson, committee papers written in jargon, situations of 'them' and 'us'. A confident, experienced community group will be ready to plan different ways of meeting with officials. One of these is to invite representatives of public agencies to have the meeting on the premises of the group because then the group can control the environment – the seating arrangement, refreshments and so on – and also influence how people will participate in the meeting.

Using bold and imaginative methods is a hallmark of community development. It seeks to tap into the creativity and energy to be found within communities. Often there is a close link between community development and community arts. CEBSD's Irish member, Combat Poverty Agency, uses the phrase "developmental community arts" to capture the idea of a group, through arts and cultural activities, expressing views on and influencing the processes that shape people's everyday lives.

The practice implications of the principle of creative and innovative organisation can be summarised as follows:

- Develop a range of organisational methods, offering the hope of change and inclusion.
- Use organisational methods that combine neighbourhood development and broader social and economic development.
- Choose organisational methods that facilitate cooperation.

We have summarised four major complex principles that underpin community development work in the context of social exclusion. They are lodged in a holistic, generic approach to working with communities, an approach that always seeks to work with people 'in the round' rather than putting them into categories. As discussed in Chapter Two, it is for this reason that community development is characterised by strategies that work across a range of issues and with a variety of organisations.

In putting forward the principles, we do not underestimate the challenging nature of the problem. Communities in which social exclusion has become a dominant factor can be places of fear and despair. People can turn against those who appear to be different – hence the rise of racist or bigoted movements in poor areas. Violence and conflict can often be near the surface, sometimes breaking out into attacks or riots. The community development approach in such areas is to plant seeds of hope, to support what may often only be a handful of people to initiate activities and action, in brief to set in motion a long-term process of change and development. As the concluding paragraph of the report on the seminar that marked the end of CEBSD's project states:

> The study of social exclusion is all too often based either on an analysis of the failures and shortcomings of the local and national state, or on the multiple disadvantages faced by those with little access to material wealth or some combination of the two. Those who wield the deficit model are part of the problem not part of the solution. Communities face the impact of the broader picture – the social, economic and cultural factors which interact together to affect social participation and its local, national, European and global dimensions. They face that as a challenge and they have the skills and potential for development, which can help meet that challenge. Recognition of those skills and fulfilment of that potential demands creativity and accountability at every level. (CEBSD, 2004, p 29)

Tapping into people's skills and building on the potential for development is at the heart of the idea of process in community development. Essentially, it means the stages of change that a community experiences and the need for this process to be in tune with a community's rhythm, the issues it believes to be important and the pace of change that it chooses. Running through these is a strong educative element. Community workers, and those who write about community development, not surprisingly give different emphases to the idea of process (Henderson and Thomas, 2002, pp 184-7). The idea of a continuum of consciousness, along which individuals may progress, is one way of specifying the idea of process. The significant points on the continuum are:

- awareness of the self and one's position and abilities to achieve change;
- awareness of the collective aspects of a problem, in other words there are other people going through a similar situation or experience;
- awareness not just of the possibilities of collective action but also of the powerfulness of the efforts of a group as compared with those of individuals;
- awareness of the political nature of decisions made in organisations such as local authorities, partnership boards and forums;
- awareness of how the interests and concerns of one's own group relate to those of other groups in the neighbourhood, local authority or city;
- awareness and interest in broader political and socioeconomic issues, regionally, nationally and globally;
- awareness of the world that goes beyond an interest in wanting to know what is going on. The individual develops a critical appreciation of his or her position, and that of other people, in society and explores causal questions about the distribution of income, wealth, opportunities and power.

Working with the idea of a community development process is extremely testing for community workers, particularly when the need to respond to a crisis situation is evident. It requires workers to have a grounding in theories of change and development. It may also mean that they have, on occasions, to argue for its importance, especially if an organisation or funding body is giving paramount attention to targets and outputs. There is no doubt that community development has to be alert to the need to modernise itself, often using the language of planning and management theory to do so. At the same time, it has to keep hold of its own, well-established and widely experienced theory.

The community development process is not always evident, and more often than not progress is made in fits and starts – two steps forward, one step back. Increasingly, however, community development workers and their organisations are becoming more aware of the factors that make things work. It is to this question that we now turn.

Measuring change

Measurements, using both 'hard' and 'soft' data, are needed, which can show how community development practice can contribute to the following issues:

Income

- information and advocacy on welfare benefits;
- bulk buying, cooperatives and exchange schemes;
- increased income resulting from community enterprises;
- savings resulting from credit unions.

Employment

- people move from unemployment to employment;
- new jobs are created;
- availability of training places.

Health and environment

- improved physical environment;
- better public health;
- increased uptake of services and facilities.

Groups and networks

- how often people meet and the composition of groups;
- members of communities feel valued and respected;
- group development;
- factors and organisation methods that influence group 'chemistry' negatively and positively;
- sense of happiness, well-being and security;
- ability to respond to new problems;
- recognition of knowledge and skills acquired in informal settings;
- visibility and voices of all members of communities;
- influence that members of communities have on specific changes.

Individuals

- individual development over the long term: self-confidence, capacity to engage with others.

Role of community development workers

- measuring the quality of the intervention – "have we done a good job?";
- level of responsibility for success and failure;
- methods of achieving cooperation.

These measurements reflect the contexts of the individuals involved in CEBSD's project. The emphasis given to groups and networks should be noted. Different contexts – work undertaken, for example, in a sparsely populated rural area – would produce a different list. Overall, however, the measurements recorded provide a good indication of what community development sets out to achieve.

In order to collect evidence about the measurements, community development programmes and projects need to develop direct measures or indirect indicators of change. This is a key stage in the evaluation model devised by the Scottish Community Development Centre:

> *A measure* is a quantified description of outputs or performances. Measures apply where there is a clear and direct relationship between the way in which the inputs are applied, the outputs they produce and outcomes that result. Cause and effect can be clearly traced.

> *An indicator* is a proxy measure used when output or performance is not directly measurable. Indicators apply where cause and effect cannot be so clearly traced. Indicators suggest, but do not prove a causal relationship – there may be many other influences involved. Evidence that a causal relationship exists is reinforced when several indicators suggest the same explanation. They relate closely to the elements, and enable assessment of whether and how change is occurring in relation to a given element. (Barr and Hashagen, 2000, p 68)

I used a modified version of this model when evaluating Sharing Voices Bradford, one of the projects that was involved with the Bradford working group in CEBSD's project. It provides an example of what is meant by measures and indicators. For the project's objectives of (a) stimulating voluntary sector activity in the area of mental health and minority ethnic communities and (b) developing capacity within communities and supporting the development of self-help/support groups and networks, the project team agreed the following measures and indicators:

Quantitative (outputs)

- number of groups supported by project staff and the issues raised;
- number of groups set up by project staff and the purpose of the groups;
- number of volunteers supported by project staff and specification of the work undertaken by the volunteers.

Qualitative (outcomes)

- interest expressed by members of community groups in engaging with mental health issues;
- observed self-confidence of members of community groups and volunteers in group situations;
- satisfaction expressed by groups and volunteers in their community activity and involvement.

It proved possible to collect good data using these measures and indicators. Particularly useful was the idea of an indicator being a proxy measure: several indicators could be connected with the project's activities, and this could be taken as evidence that the project was being effective. A single indicator was not enough.

Specifying measures and indicators requires time and patience and needs to be undertaken with all of those organisations and groups that are, or will be, involved in a community development project. The indicators will emerge as a result of having identified the key factors that reflect particular principles and practice. For example, the factors that relate to the principle of equality, diversity and tolerance will be members of communities feeling valued and respected, the visibility and voices of all community members, the composition of the groups and a group's capacity to engage with others.

Planning, evaluating and learning from community development interventions in the context of social exclusion are of critical importance. The Scottish model referred to earlier in this chapter is one way of approaching the issue. In England, the Home Office and the Audit Commission have supported in-depth work by the Community Development Foundation (CDF) on ways of knowing when a community is flourishing and how this can be measured (see Chanan, 2004). CDF is currently testing, with a number of

These pictures show local people experiencing training courses at the Civil College, Kunbabony, Hungary. The college was set up by the Hungarian Association for Community Development.

Young people in the Cape Verdean neighbourhood of Cova da Moura, on the outskirts of Lisbon, Portugal. The youth programme is a cornerstone in the neighbourhood's renewal.

organisations, four indicators of community involvement: community influence, community cohesion, social capital and the condition of the community and voluntary sector (Humm et al, 2004).

Participatory action-research models used in developing countries, and now being applied in European countries, are another important source. It is clear that measuring change is now widely accepted – by community groups as well as practitioners and managers – as being an essential part of community development responses to social exclusion. It is also clear that there are the methodological tools available to undertake rigorous evaluation.

Community groups in Flanders exchange ideas and experiences on the development of neighbourhoods, facilitated by community development workers.

Some of the participants at the Berlin seminar (2003), which discussed the findings of CEBSD's good practice project (see Chapter One).

FIVE

Common understandings

Throughout Europe there is a revival of community development, not only in those countries that have a long tradition in the field but also in countries such as Bulgaria, Romania and the Czech Republic. The political climate is favourable because governments, and increasing numbers of local authorities, are promoting interactive management in which citizens are involved in the early stages of decision making. A key question facing European, national, regional and local community development organisations, given the favourable climate, turns on the definition and meaning of community development being used: is there a common understanding of community development in the European context? The question is of crucial importance if community development is to make a serious contribution, at the level of policy as well as practice, to social inclusion programmes.

The following analysis is based partly on literature and partly on the report of a survey carried out among the 10 members of CEBSD (Hautekeur, 2004). While there is no one uniform definition of community development among CEBSD's membership, the following key concepts are highlighted in the definitions of at least two or more of the members. Community development:

- delivers professional and independent support to groups of people;
- identifies, together with local people, community problems;
- increases the empowerment of local people so that they can organise themselves in order to solve problems;
- turns its attention primarily to people struggling with social deprivation and exclusion;
- contributes to a sustainable community based on mutual respect and social justice;
- challenges power structures that hinder people's participation;
- contributes to the sociocultural development of the neighbourhood by local people.

Similarities and differences

The diversity of community development across Europe reflects, in the first instance, the different organisational contexts of individual countries and regions. In 2000, the national Social Cultural Office in the Netherlands made a comparison of a number of European countries. It found that the Netherlands and the Scandinavian countries are characterised by a high level of organisation in civil society. At the other end of the spectrum, we find that France and other Southern European countries have a low level of organisation. The remaining countries of Western Europe are somewhere in the middle.

In Central and Eastern Europe, the connections between civil society and community development remain of central importance. As we shall see, this reached an important staging post at an international conference held in Budapest in 2004. Vercseg's analysis of the Central and Eastern European region underlines the complexity of the situation: "We can say that some of the organisations in the region tackle this complexity by defining community development as an independent profession while others apply it mainly as a method of community improvement" (Vercseg, 2003). She argues that the emergence of community development as a professional field can be linked directly to democracy and the emergence of civil society. She also, however, expresses doubts as to whether community development can become more broadly recognised within Central and Eastern European countries. This is primarily because support from national systems and programmes has not been forthcoming.

In addition to the differences of organisation of civil society across Europe, there are also large differences in welfare systems. A study comparing the Netherlands and Portugal found that, in the Netherlands there is a relatively high level of services provided. Futhermore, community development has obtained its own terrain and role. In Portugal, on the other hand, basic social services are incomplete and little attention is given to the collective involvement of local people. The professional status of community development is low (Van den Hoven, 2002).

Some countries have community development workers and similar professionals whereas such people are not to be found in others. The meaning of the Anglo-Saxon concept of community development is more or less synonymous with the understanding of community development in Flanders (Belgium) and the Netherlands. The Centre for Community Work and Mobilisation (CESAM) in Sweden is also inspired by this model. In Southern European countries, the term 'social development' is used to describe developmental or development-orientated activities. The French organisation is called Le Mouvement pour un Développement Social Local. In France, 'community' has different connotations and significance to how it is used in the UK. Each culture has its own echoes of the word, especially in former Soviet bloc countries.

The findings of CEBSD's survey point to border lines in the welfare and community development landscape between Northern and Southern Europe. This picture, however, requires nuancing. In Italy, for example, there is no tradition of community development yet cooperatives have widespread support. Moreover, not all Northern European countries have the same understanding of a collective and participatory approach. *Gemeinwesenarbeit* (community development) in Germany is not widespread. In Belgium, although in Flanders there are well-developed structures for community development that are subsidised by the Flemish government, in Wallonia, in the southern part of the country, community development is non-existent.

CEBSD members were asked to locate themselves on the diagram in Figure 5.1. Horizontally, they were to indicate whether the organisation focused on support to elected council members or Members of Parliament (representative democracy) or whether their principal concern was to support local community organisations (participatory democracy). Vertically, they were asked to indicate

Figure 5.1: Priorities for action (CEBSD)

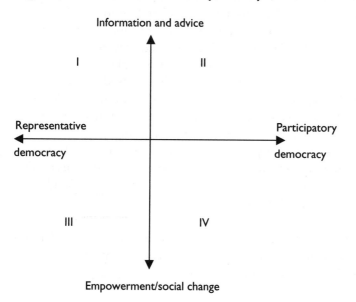

whether the organisation focused on information and advice to citizens in the context of government programmes or whether they gave priority to support of local community groups. The aim of the latter is to strengthen target groups (empowerment) in the light of the desired societal transformations.

All members gave priority to participatory democracy and the empowerment of local people (quadrant IV). At the same time, various members pointed out that in their daily work the image was more complex. Thus Desenvolupament Comunitari in Catalonia noted that many of the local authorities with which it works have a limited concept of citizens' participation. For them it is the same as information and consultation. CDF in the UK stressed that, in practice, it is involved in all four quadrants.

Many of CEBSD's members pointed, in the survey, to the following issues as priorities: participation, strengthening civil society and local democracy, employment opportunities, housing, improvement of neighbourhoods, social inclusion, sustainable development, rural development, diversity, intercultural mediation and communication. The members have different emphases. The Combat Poverty Agency in Ireland, for example, sees community development as a major tool in the struggle against poverty. CESAM in Sweden is in the forefront of promoting active citizenship and democratic decision making. The Ideas Bank in Norway sees its priority as facilitating dialogue between local people and the authorities on the issue of sustainable development. The Hungarian Association for Community Development connects community development strongly with adult education.

Yet despite the differing national or regional contexts, the member organisations of CEBSD have achieved a high degree of agreement with regard to the basic purposes and principles of community development. A common term or guideline used is community development as a bottom-up process in which common problems are approached collectively in a participatory manner. Empowerment of community groups and structural change are central to this. As well as showing that community development can take place and grow in different political and cultural contexts, the survey also indicates that whether or not community development goes forward depends on a combination of the following:

- a recognition of autonomous community groups and organisations and of a definite community development discipline;
- financial support from government;

- an openness towards interactive or participative decision making processes;
- a greater awareness among policy makers of the added value of community development;
- a core community development curriculum in higher education programmes;
- high-quality training and solid research for practitioners;
- bringing groups together to exchange and disseminate good practice;
- inter-regional and international links between community development organisations in a European framework.

Community development's effectiveness at grassroots level will depend on the strategic and tactical acumen of community groups, advised and supported at times by community development workers. As a result of the experience gained throughout Europe, groups and workers have become more sophisticated in thinking through the advantages and disadvantages of particular approaches. Harry Salmon, for example, suggests the following as a guideline:

> If the main aim for the socially excluded is to achieve goals that are to do with the smoother and more appropriate delivery of services, information, access to agencies etc., then it is tactically wise to employ normal consultative processes including representation on appropriate groups, committees etc. However, if the aim is to achieve changes involving significant redistribution of resources and changes in policies, then the tactics will draw upon community action traditions as well as more consensual approaches. In the first, the socially excluded would make use of existing administrative and consultative procedures; but in the second, the focus would be on exerting political pressures. This rough distinction could apply to action at different levels from the local to the European. (Salmon, personal communication)

The Budapest Declaration

The extent to which a common understanding of community development among the member organisations of CEBSD is emerging was confirmed at an important conference entitled Building European Civil Society through Community Development. It was held in

Budapest in March 2004 and was organised by CEBSD, the Hungarian Association for Community Development and the International Association for Community Development. The 130 participants (from 33 countries) reached an agreement on key community development principles and priorities. The resulting document, known as the Budapest Declaration (see Appendix A), has been disseminated widely and has been received positively by the European Union (EU), Council of Europe and other organisations.

The Declaration provides a framework for community development internationally. It is especially important in the European context because of the links being made between community development organisations in the enlarged EU. The key issues worked on by the conference were:

- policy and legislation
- training
- theory and research
- rural issues
- urban regeneration
- sustainable development and the environment
- lifelong learning and cultural development
- local economic development and the social economy
- minorities, racism and discrimination.

These are the substantive areas on which community development organisations, at different levels, will be working in the coming years. Organisations will need to identify the specific contribution that community development can make to each area, based on the experiences of communities and the community development process. They will also need to communicate the outcomes to policy makers.

One of the most critical points of discussion during the debate on the Budapest Declaration was how far community development should be given a strong link with tackling social exclusion. Those participants who favoured the link argued that it gives community development a specific focus and commitment. Those who had reservations about the link preferred to think of community development as needing to work with all members of a community on a range of possible issues: they were concerned that connecting it too strongly with social exclusion would mean it could end up working with only one section of the community. While both of these perspectives were incorporated into the Declaration, the debate had particular relevance to CEBSD's preparation of this publication. It underlined the importance of keeping discussion about community development principles alive and open. Community development is a contested concept: those people who are involved in it debate its meaning because community development changes and because people come to it from a range of ideological and professional perspectives – the phrase 'a broad church' is used sometimes to describe the variety of opinions held and the importance, nevertheless, of talking about these within a shared framework of community development values and principles. Community development stays relevant to people's lives precisely because it is dynamic, responding to communities' priorities and the changing policy context. We return to this theme in the concluding chapter.

Implications

If the experiences of CEBSD's member organisations and the Budapest Declaration provide a basis for taking forward a common understanding of community development – particularly in the context of civil society – the implications for groups and organisations at the local, regional, national and European levels are considerable. Here we identify the key actors at the various levels:

Local level

- community groups
- community leaders (chairperson, secretary and so on)
- neighbourhood centres
- informal networks of local people
- community development workers
- other practitioners, for example youth workers, health workers, planners, regeneration officers
- managers
- councillors (local elected members) and local government officers.

Regional level (within a country)

- regional offices of national government
- regional organisations
- regional offices of non-governmental organisations
- elected regional bodies
- regional community development organisations
- regional training and education organisations.

National level

- national government – all ministries/departments
- elected members
- non-governmental organisations
- campaigning organisations.

European level

- networks of residents and practitioners
- non-governmental organisations (networks), such as CEBSD, the European Anti-Poverty Network (EAPN)
- intergovernmental organisations – the EU, Council of Europe.

These are the groups, networks and organisations that need to be involved in taking forward the community development agenda. In the next chapter, we outline the kinds of action that are required.

SIX

Agenda for action

As part of its centenary events, the Joseph Rowntree Foundation, a major UK trust, invited Bruce Katz of the Brookings Institution in the US to give a paper entitled *Neighbourhoods of choice and connection*. The speaker reviewed American neighbourhood policy and suggested what this means for the UK's social exclusion policies. He had some positive points to make about work at neighbourhood level, even suggesting that the 'neighbourhood effects literature' probably underestimates the economic and social assets of these communities: "Proximity to nodes of employment and key infrastructure, as well as the existence of such key institutions as community groups, churches and informal support networks, likely provide important support to neighbourhood residents that have yet to be fully assessed" (Katz, 2004, p 12).

Katz's analysis, however, also makes some critical comments about neighbourhood work, including that generally it has ignored core issues of household poverty as defined by access to good jobs and the accumulation of wealth. A strong argument is put for *locating* neighbourhood-based programmes in the wider metropolitan or regional context and for involving the private sector in addition to the non-governmental sector.

Such a critique of the core basis or platform of community development reminds us of the need to restate the case for mobilising and organising local people at neighbourhood level (around social, cultural and environmental issues as well as economic ones). It also, however, challenges those people and organisations involved in community development to invest time and energy in reviewing it. This means, in the first place, not making assumptions that community development is inherently virtuous and, second, being prepared to examine the evidence relating to its effectiveness and thus to be prepared to change direction. This means, in turn, that there is a case for community development having a strong policy dimension: policy makers need to hear from communities, community development workers and their organisations about what does and does not work. This is especially important when community development sets out to have an impact on situations of social exclusion.

.y questions are: How do you get policy makers to listen to
.ssages arising from the experiences of community development?
can communities influence policy? How do policy responses to
.ial exclusion change? In most European countries, community
.evelopment has performed weakly on this issue compared with its
successes of working with community groups and networks. There is,
accordingly, still some way to go in understanding and strengthening
the connections between grassroots community development and
policy formulation. In this publication, we are particularly concerned
with the European policy context. First, however, we shall return to
the three other levels summarised at the end of the Chapter Five.
What are the action implications, in policy terms, for the groups and
organisations listed?

Local

The most exciting aspect of CEBSD's EU-funded project was the
connections of common language and solidarity forged between the
residents and community development workers involved. The
experience was an example of an important theme within community
development, namely that while most community development takes
place in particular neighbourhoods and communities of interest, the
issues and challenges are the same or similar across neighbourhoods
and communities of interest. The need for groups and workers,
therefore, to have confirmation of community development principles
and priorities is clear. It is crucial that people do not feel themselves
to be on their own.

Being part of local, regional, national and European networks means
that committed residents and workers can obtain support from people
outside their immediate area or constituency who are involved in
similar kinds of projects and actions. It also provides an important
basis for mutual learning so that individuals become more confident
and skilled and groups' human resources are strengthened.

In a sense, community groups and workers always need to face in
two directions: towards their constituencies and potential sources of
support in communities, and towards policy makers. The dialogue
with the latter needs to be about the messages and demands arising
from the activities and actions of communities, but it also needs to be
about how the level of activities and actions can be sustained: resources
are needed to enable groups and workers to make connections with
other projects and organisations. In that way, they have the chance to
be part of a wider movement.

Local authorities are the key target group for community groups to engage with. In addition to supporting the local work of groups, they can be asked to fund links with a range of other groups. Employment, health and environmental organisations can also be approached. In the UK, for example, health agencies have become significant funders of community development. Community development's agenda with local authorities and other agencies is particularly demanding because of the range of issues that can be raised. For example, a local authority that commits itself to having a policy and strategy on community development is also likely to need to develop effective neighbourhood management systems.

Regional

In a number of European countries, the role and responsibilities of regional agencies and the regional arms of government have grown in significance. They have resources that can be used to support community development and, because of their intermediary position between the local and the national levels, they are well positioned to influence national decision making. In the UK, regional government offices and regional development agencies have been established relatively recently and are examples of this system. In France, there has been a commitment to regionalisation for even longer.

There is scope for strengthening the regional organisation of community development. In England, a number of national community development organisations, such as the Federation for Community Development Learning, work on a regional basis. Separate structures and networks exist for community development in the other three countries of the UK. In the Flemish part of Belgium and Brussels, the Flemish government provides a grant for a national community development organisation (VIBOSO) and eight regional institutes for community development work (RISOs). Regional institutes have been set up in Antwerp, Ghent and Brussels and in the five Flemish provinces.

Community groups, usually working through a regional or sub-regional membership organisation, need to build links with regional government and development agencies so that the latter are informed about activities and action at community level. The economic remit of many regional agencies means that community groups will need to communicate to policy makers how community involvement can underpin economic and regeneration programmes.

National

Community development organisations at all levels have become increasingly aware of the importance of engaging with national policy agendas. For example, the Swedish member of CEBSD, CESAM, has made the case to politicians for a national framework in Sweden. It organised a visit to London so that the politicians could hear from the UK member, CDF, how a national community development organisation works. The importance of having this dimension is especially evident when governments commit themselves to major social inclusion, regeneration, urban renewal and rural development programmes that include a significant community development element. The UK-wide survey of community development workers referred to in Chapter Two picked up this point, drawing attention to the apparent lack of understanding and recognition of community development practice in policy documents and programme guidelines: "The community development work profession must take further the commitment to addressing some of the weaknesses and problems that have been identified. It needs to articulate both the practice and the employment-related requirements more effectively" (Glen et al, 2004, p 60).

In any one country, ways need to be found for community development to have well-coordinated and accountable structures that can keep pace with and influence the policy agenda. Sometimes a federated structure of regional and national community development organisations will be appropriate. In other contexts, such as in Ireland and the UK, models have developed in which community development has both a statutory or semi-statutory presence at the policy table and one based on membership organisations.

Two key areas must underpin work undertaken on policy. The first is the capacity within community development to sustain an overview nationally of trends and developments. In those countries, for example, in which community development has been recognised and resourced by local authorities, it is essential that the strategies of local authorities as a whole are monitored and evaluated. An absence of this kind of work would result in the isolation of community development within particular areas, with the likelihood that practitioners and managers would become inward-looking and resistant to change.

The second essential component of the national element is the sharing and dissemination of good practice on community development. The initiative, mentioned in Chapter Two, on weak community infrastructures in Northern Ireland is a good example of how the development of good practice can be shared and taken forward into the policy arena. The community development partnership building programme in Central and Eastern Europe (2001–03) is a second striking example of exchange and development. It involved organisations from Hungary, Poland, Slovakia and Romania and was concerned essentially with training the trainers: a series of pilot training courses and action designed to disseminate ideas and examples of community development in the region; also of encouraging cooperation and long-term partnerships. This kind of exchange brought to the attention of participants those traditions and practices held in common in the region, rather than the opposite. The Hungarian, Romanian and Polish organisations, for example, all have strong contact with cultural houses, although they are at different phases. Cultural houses, which promote democratic traditions and practice and provide an experimental field for developing new professions, represent an interesting type of institution in the region. The flow of information about this kind of initiative, in order that others can learn from it, needs to be a high priority for community development in the national context.

European

Case study

The following case study describes the experience of European Anti-Poverty Network (EAPN) Ireland (an active member of EAPN) in encouraging local anti-poverty groups to engage with the development of the proposed new EU Constitution and the educational and mobilising opportunities that this offered. The main focus of EAPN Ireland has been on the EU's anti-poverty strategy but work on this has been hampered by the lack of legal basis for the strategy.

Ireland has, historically, a poor record in social policy, with the highest rate of 'relative poverty' and some of the worst public services in the EU. Ireland was one of the minority of countries that blocked the inclusion of an enforceable Charter of Fundamental Rights in the Nice Treaty. On the other hand, Ireland has often promoted important initiatives in EU social policy, as far back as the Poverty I programme in the 1970s. Later Irish governments proposed the clause in the Amsterdam Treaty that provides the basis of the anti-poverty strategy, and the clause in the Nice Treaty giving status to the Social Protection Committee that drives the strategy.

The fact that every new treaty must go to referendum in Ireland means that there is more discussion than in many other countries, although this discussion is often simplistic. In a referendum, the only choice is to say 'yes' to the whole treaty, which few want to do, or to say 'no', threatening to unravel the whole deal. This is why EAPN Ireland has always preferred to focus on the negotiations leading to treaties.

The National Forum on Europe is a major opportunity for this. It was set up after the defeat of the Nice Treaty in the 2001 referendum, with a mandate to discuss all aspects of Ireland's role in the EU. It is run by the parties in the Oireachtas (Parliament) and includes in the discussions an 'observer pillar' made up of social partners, non-governmental organisations, pro- and anti-Nice campaigns, small parties and churches. EAPN Ireland has been one of the most active members of this 'pillar' from the start.

Learning and mobilising

As well as weekly discussions on EU–Ireland issues, the Forum has run several 'rounds' of local public meetings. The first two rounds, of about 20 meetings, were held in January and October 2002 with politicians and sometimes non-governmental organisation speakers.

EAPN Ireland decided to use these as an opportunity to link local groups to EU discussions. As soon as the dates and venues for public meetings were announced, member groups were contacted in each town, looking for 'hosts' for small seminars for anti-poverty groups on the same day. These were usually held from 4–6pm, with sandwiches for those who stayed for the Forum public meetings at 8pm. This formula was followed over the next two years, as the Constitution and the Forum moved on. More than 35 local discussions were organised, with over 600 participants, over a period of three years.

The local hosts were sometimes individual groups, such as Traveller support groups or community groups, but were more often local community 'platforms' bringing together most anti-poverty groups in the area. The agenda was planned jointly, but in most cases followed a fairly standard 'template', with small local variations.

The seminars were promoted locally by the hosts and nationally by EAPN Ireland with the support of other national anti-poverty networks and organisations. The seminars discussed the key poverty and rights issues in the Constitution, and EAPN Ireland encouraged anti-poverty groups to take these up in the evening Forum meetings. There was a lot of enthusiasm for this but, in the event, while some spoke, many were intimidated by the seemingly more informed political activists.

This meant that the more participative seminars were especially important spaces for more relaxed discussion.

Campaigning

The Convention on the Future of Europe, which brought together representatives of national parliaments and governments to discuss a thorough revision of the Nice Treaty, and later a draft EU Constitution, was the most open such process ever. It produced a quantity of information and proposals and often left little time for lobbying on particular points. To lobby effectively, it was vital to be able to digest and disseminate this information.

The *act4europe campaign* is a European contact group focusing on civil society. It links social, environmental, development and human rights non-governmental organisations and the trades unions. It was vital to handling this information, building on the experience of long cooperation between the European Social Platform and the trades unions to promote the Charter of Fundamental Rights. The campaign produced background 'toolkits', regular updates and urgent action appeals, which EAPN Ireland was able to adapt and use.

Members and supporters were encouraged to write letters and e-mails on a number of occasions during the Convention and the subsequent Inter Governmental Conference (IGC). These often led to meetings with key politicians. They also helped remind politicians and officials, who saw the same two staff members at weekly national Forum meetings, that there was a strong and interested membership behind the ideas being put forward. The withdrawal of Ireland's effective veto on an enforceable Charter of Fundamental Rights may have been partly the result of the often monotonous repetition by EAPN Ireland members at local Forum meetings of the importance of the Charter, persuading government politicians that opposing the Charter could cause them more embarrassment than supporting it.

After a lobbying and media campaign, the Taoiseach (Prime Minister) agreed, at a Forum meeting, to table an amendment to ensure that social inclusion must be taken into account in all EU policies at the IGC. This was accepted by the IGC and could potentially be a powerful legal tool to bring trade, monetary, budgetary and other policies into some balance, although the actual implementation will involve another political push.

Lessons

What did EAPN Ireland learn?

- There is an interest in EU issues among local activists, who can see the importance of the issues but who find it hard to get appropriate, accessible and timely information and to know how and when to intervene.
- The combination of clear aims and flexibility to constantly rethink strategy was effective but is not always possible in funded projects. EAPN Ireland was fortunate to have funding from the Combat Poverty Agency and later the Department of Community, Rural and Gaeltacht Affairs under the National Anti-Poverty Networks Programme that allowed this flexibility.
- With hindsight, it might have been better to bring more explicit proposals to the seminars on issues to take up in the public meetings. In trying not to be prescriptive, and to encourage debate, members may not have been provided with clear-enough speaking points.
- The work was a big drain on the resources of a small organisation, with only three staff. It was worthwhile because of the training and consciousness-raising, although the actual policy impact on the ground remains to be seen.
- Local events had a good turn-out, particularly in medium-sized towns, in a way that national or regional events seldom do. This may be because there are so many national and regional events to choose from, but few locally. It may also be that local meetings are more relaxed and less off-putting.
- The Forum provided a vital space for discussion (see www.forumoneurope.ie). (Robin Hanan, Coordinator EAPN Ireland – see www.eapn.org)

This example of lobbying at the European policy level is unusual in community development. For the most part, community development organisations do not have the capability to pursue this route. It needs, however, to be kept open as an option, to form part of a wider strategy. Alongside a lobbying role, for example, is the need for organisations to be kept informed about European Commission programmes that relate to community development. While some of these, such as the Social Inclusion Programme and the LEADER+ programme for rural areas, are self-evident, others may be less so. The 1999-2002 local social capital programme, for example, which operated under Article 6 of the European Social Fund, had considerable implications for community development and was researched for the European Anti-Poverty Network (Harvey, 2003). This meant that other European networks, such as CEBSD, could learn from the experience and could include knowledge about it in their discussions with the Commission.

Engaging with European policy makers, usually via Commission staff, should ideally take place while a programme is running, rather than leaving it to the end. The need to provide inputs on the key issue of indicators in the Social Inclusion Programme illustrates this point well. By working in partnership with other networks, again in this case with EAPN because of research it has undertaken on the issue, CEBSD can help to ensure that the views and experiences of excluded groups and communities are communicated to the Commission and acted on. Many of the European non-governmental organisations and networks active on the issue of social exclusion work together through their membership of the European Social Platform, which meets regularly with the Commission. It provides an important access point for community development organisations.

Lobbying and engaging in dialogue with the Commission, the Council of Europe and other European bodies are skilled and highly demanding in terms of staff time. When representatives of the partner organisations involved in CEBSD's project reconvened in Brussels in 2004, they worked on the question of how to influence policy makers, particularly on how policy can help practice move forward. There was an awareness of the need for community development organisations to recognise and understand the context in which policy is made. The formulation of national action plans is central to the wider European policy-making process and both regional and national community development organisations should aim to be involved in discussions of the plans. At the European level, it is essential to open up this dimension in partnership with non-governmental and other networks, especially the women's lobby, social economy networks and the youth sector. The point was also made that the findings of action-research, carried out in collaboration with universities, can also be effective in influencing policy.

However, it was the more unusual ideas discussed at the Brussels conference that received most attention: face-to-face meetings between local people and policy makers, exchanges and visits of local people between different countries, the availability of the experiences of community groups in a variety of forms, such as short case studies, videos and presentations by groups. The experiences should be told in ways that capture the realities of working in and with communities: the high points and the low ones, victories and disappointments – as much can be learned from practice that has not worked as from that which has.

Community groups and community development workers are right to pose the question: Why should we be part of the wider, European context? How can this context connect with local action? The importance of sharing good practice is the main reason why the wider picture is important but, on the basis of CEBSD's experience, we can add the following:

- Many of the issues are the same or similar and people can learn from each other as to how to tackle them; this includes skills and participation techniques (for example Planning for Real, the technique developed to maximise the involvement of local people in decision making) as well as strategies.
- Learning and inspiration can happen not only through action and practice but also through ideas. Thus, the way in which the concept of civil society has been developed in Central and Eastern European countries has influenced those people involved in community development in other parts of Europe.
- Being open to the wider context can help to explain and illustrate some of the language surrounding community development, for example capacity building, community cohesion and social capital.
- It helps identify emerging themes for community development to address; the relevance of social capital theory is an example.
- It helps give a sense of perspective as to what can be achieved by communities.

The strongest recommendation from the discussion at CEBSD's Brussels conference was for community development organisations, when operating in policy situations, to consider using methods of organising meetings similar to those used with communities: avoid formal meetings, plan them so that they combine serious debate with social activity, try to ensure the maximum participation of all those present. A method called Café Dialogue was used, very effectively, in CEBSD's project at both the Berlin seminar (which brought the project to an end) and the reconvening of participants at the Brussels conference.

The method requires the room to be set up as a café: tables with paper cloths (on which people are encouraged to write), a tape for playing popular music and a lot of movement of the participants between the tables. Each table is assigned one issue and a facilitator stays there for each round of the 'dialogue' that is played: each time the music stops, participants discuss the named issue, encouraged by the facilitators to build on the comments of the participants from the previous rounds. At the end of three or four rounds, each of the facilitators summarises on a flip chart the main points that have emerged and gives feedback on it to all the participants. It is a quick, enjoyable and effective way of developing new ideas. It also ensures that everyone in the room is fully involved. (For fuller information, contact CEBSD's member in Norway – The Ideas Bank.)

Methods such as Café Dialogue have been developed extensively by practitioners across Europe in recent years. Their informality and careful structuring have been shown to produce clear, often imaginative outcomes from meetings, and they encourage the involvement of everyone. There is every reason why such methods should be used in the policy context, rather than restricting them to work with communities and practitioners.

Supporting visits of residents and community development workers to projects, neighbourhoods and organisations in other countries is important for a number of reasons. Often the visits can be combined with participation in a national or European conference. Visits can be inspiring for those involved and, provided full feedback is given, helpful to community groups. The funding priorities of trusts can be scrutinised to identify potential funding sources. The Commission has schemes that can assist visits and exchanges. But these ways of exchanging and developing good practice are surely important too for another reason: do they not give a signal to policy makers that local people must be recognised as players or stakeholders in Europe's engagement with the issue of social exclusion? We explore this and related points in Chapter Seven.

The scope for community development organisations working in the European context is considerable. There is a need to ensure that the principles and practice that have been identified in this publication connect with policy making. Otherwise, through lack of recognition and resourcing, the potential of community development's contribution to combating social exclusion will not be realised.

SEVEN

Conclusions

> At the core is that Roma express their own opinions, take
> their own decisions and act themselves. In the community
> development approach Roma formulate their own issues
> and also the possible solutions.... Only if Roma have been
> empowered and have built up their own organisations,
> might they become partners in society and gain more power
> and influence. In this process, Roma become stronger while
> influencing policy. It is very important that Roma leaders
> keep in close contact with the local people. The base of
> the movement always stays at the local level. (Schuringa,
> 2005, pp 3-4)

The author of the publication from which this statement is taken goes
on to argue for the importance also of uniting the Roma in national
and international networks. A strategic decision to work at several
different levels is of central importance in work undertaken to include
the excluded through community development. The need for a
multilevel strategy provides the overarching principle behind the
following six key themes or priorities that can be drawn out of the
preceding chapters. In most, if not all, instances the phrase 'unfinished
business' needs to be inserted alongside each theme. We have drawn
attention to the energy and resourcefulness of people across Europe
who are committed to community development and social inclusion,
and we have outlined an agenda for action. In this concluding chapter,
we consider ways in which community development itself has to
change.

Intercultural community development

The situation faced by Roma in several Central and Eastern European
countries forms part of a Europe-wide phenomenon of discrimination,
racism and xenophobia experienced by migrants, refugees, asylum
seekers and members of minority ethnic groups. It is crucial that
community development continues to engage with the issue,
particularly in the context of social exclusion. This requires

organisations to understand the nature of the oppression and discrimination experienced by these different groups and to develop critiques and strategies that recognise the differences between the groups. There are, for instance, few policies specifically for refugees and asylum seekers; instead policies designed originally to meet the needs of economic migrants have been used towards refugees and asylum seekers.

Ruth Lister points out that, in both developed and developing countries, poverty is racially and ethnically patterned: "non-White groups are disproportionately likely to be poor in White-dominated societies, and immigrants, asylum-seekers, Roma and indigenous peoples are particularly vulnerable to poverty" (Lister, 2004, p 62). The exploitation of migrants in the labour market has been documented widely by researchers and journalists.

For community development, the racism resulting from the global economic system is all too frequently played out in those communities that are most excluded – inner-city neighbourhoods and public housing estates. It is wrong to imagine, however, that racism does not take place in other kinds of communities too, including rural areas. For example, in a booklet on community development responses to rural racism, the title of one of the case studies is 'We shoot them at Newark!'. This is a reference to attitudes by some White residents towards members of minority ethnic groups in one of England's most rural counties, Lincolnshire (Craig et al, 1999, p 22).

Serious engagement with multicultural Europe requires there to be a new phase in the history of community development. It needs to rest on a determination to convince politicians, policy makers and agencies to understand and respect the needs of minority ethnic groups, asylum seekers and refugees. This is a key entry point for the multiculturalism advocated by Tariq Modood and the "emerging recognition that multiculturalism means a new way of being French, a new way of being German, a new way of being British – and perhaps a new way of being European" (Modood, 1997, p 24). It means that a more plural approach to racial disadvantage needs to be developed that can lead to the formulation of an explicit and appropriate ideal of multicultural citizenship. It is an approach that welcomes difference and diversity and it is an approach that requires strong opposition to the policies and practices of extreme right-wing groups that attack – verbally and physically – members of minority ethnic groups, refugees and asylum seekers.

In a paper prepared for the 2004 Budapest conference, the director of Desenvolupament Comunitari, Carles Riera, argues that a new model for responding to the multicultural context is needed:

> Up to this point, two models of migration incorporation have been developed in Europe: assimilation (coming from the French tradition) and multiculturalism (more usual in Anglo–Saxon contexts). In the first case, diversity has been sacrificed in the name of equality. In the second case, diversity and segregation have been legitimised by assuming inequality. Since inclusion and equality have not been achieved, both models have failed. (Riera, 2005: forthcoming)

The author goes on to argue that a new model, in the context of community development, needs to be based on equality of opportunities, the prevention of urban segregation and on valuing and respecting diversity in a shared framework of coexistence. The work undertaken in Barcelona on intercultural mediation aims to move closer to the formulation of an inclusive intercultural model of community development.

A 'new' community development needs to cast off the 'old' traditions of Anglo–Saxon, French and Dutch community development: look for new alliances, try out different ways of working but, above all, be prepared to listen closely to the voices of those people who, because of who they are, live in the shadow of mainstream society. The practice that has developed so far, examples of which have been mentioned earlier, is important. Now it has to be taken further.

Maintaining community development's breadth

The breadth of community development can refer to at least three phenomena:

1. The range of issues that are addressed by communities. In this publication we have focused on social exclusion and regeneration but underneath these issues is an enormous variety of actions and activities on, for example: children's play, community safety, facilities for young people, community care, sport, the environment, drugs prevention and community education.
2. The extent to which different disciplines are brought to bear on issues and problems in communities, and consequently the range

of professions that are involved in community development; for example social work, economic development, youth work, housing, planning.

3. How the concept of community development is understood and interpreted by different organisations and policies. It is this meaning that is discussed here.

The interest being shown in community development by a number of European governments is to be welcomed. Much of it stems from the commitment being made to regenerate deprived, mainly urban, areas. The UK government has targeted resources at these areas, at the same time insisting that regeneration programmes be run in partnership with communities. In the Netherlands, Koos Vos notes that the large cities have been given increased freedom to develop renewal policies: "The cabinet proposed an even greater freedom for cities to design their own policies, enabling them to operate by focusing on results with a minimum of bureaucracy, an improved tailor-made character and on a neighbourhood-oriented approach involving even more citizens, private agencies and business" (Vos, 2005: forthcoming).

Community development organisations should respond positively to the interest in and commitment to community involvement being demonstrated by policy makers in regeneration, health, rural development and other areas. Community development, after all, has always argued for being an open profession. It has sought to encourage others to learn about it and to adapt it to their professional or other needs. It was in recognition of the extent to which this has happened that writers in the UK developed the concept of community practice. They use the term to "encompass practice that embraces, but is broader than either community work or community development, although it derives some of its methods and virtually all of its values from the traditions of community work and community development" (Banks, 2004, p 11). 'Community practice' is thus put forward as a generic term that covers the work of self-managed groups and of community workers, the work of other professionals with a community focus and the work of policy makers that is geared towards community policies and partnership working.

However, community development's argument for openness and transferability carries a hidden danger: the virtue of remaining broad and open is that community development's principles and methods can, paradoxically, be used in a narrow way. A profession or discipline can change and adapt them so radically that their connection with community development is seriously weakened. Ilona Vercseg alerts us to this danger when reflecting on community development in the context of both social work and regional development in Hungary:

> I have seen many examples of how, within the framework of social work, even community development and community work can be narrowed down to a service providing activity instead of resulting in endogenous development and changes. Similarly, we can see how it is evolving to become a tool in the regional development profession. The ruling trend in development focuses on infrastructural development and not social development, and the principle of involving stakeholders is only a formality. The other day, a colleague burst out: "Does regional development need local people at all?" If community development becomes subordinate to any other profession there is a risk that it might lose its interdisciplinary character and independence, and those in power will use it as the means to achieve their own goals. (Vercseg, 2005, p 2)

The narrowing of community development occurs because it is made to be too functional: to service and support the policies and programmes of agencies. The more that attention is given to its functional purpose, the less scope there is to communicate its underlying values and philosophy. At the regional seminar of Central and Eastern European partners held in Romania in 2003, I suggested that there could be three possible consequences of this trend:

1. There is a possibility that in those countries, especially the UK and the Netherlands, where there are major regeneration programmes in which community development has been drawn in to support them, the identity of community development could become lost.
2. As it responds to policy makers' growing interest in 'community', there is a danger that community development will promise too much. This is because (a) the goals of regeneration programmes are very ambitious, and community development is being swept along with them and (b) community development as a profession may not be strong enough to deliver on the expectations. There is, accordingly, a danger that both policy makers and communities will become disappointed, even disillusioned, with community development.

3. A functional approach to community development is likely to pull community workers away from neighbourhoods. This is because of the dominance of the partnership approach in regeneration programmes: a range of agencies and boards working together at a level that is distant from peoples' lives in communities. (Henderson, 2003a, p 5)

Maintaining the breadth of community development needs to be on the European agenda of community development organisations. The experience of community development in large regeneration programmes, which have been running since the early 1990s, could be replicated in future social inclusion programmes. Keeping a watchful eye on how these develop, while at the same time supporting them and participating in them, needs all the political and analytical skills that community development can draw on.

New issues

It can be misleading to refer to new issues as it is nearly always possible to find ways in which a theme or issue has been worked on before. In community development, however, it is crucially important for workers, community leaders, managers, researchers and others to be alert to ways in which the world is changing around them: to be prepared to understand and engage with change. Community development, in that sense, cannot afford to live in the past. Often, indeed, it should be at the forefront of new ideas and movements and their impact on communities.

The best example of this point is the way that environmental action has come onto the agenda of community development in the European context and the rapidity with which it has made connections with health, housing and economic problems faced by communities. Fifteen years ago, it was rare to find the issue of environmental action listed at community development conferences or discussed by community workers in Europe (although not in the South). Now its importance is widely recognised, not just globally but locally. Chris Church and Charlie Garratt summarise why environmental change is important as follows:

- It can offer 'quick fixes': it can show that things are changing in an area and that something is actually happening (which can be a problem with long-term programmes).

- It can improve quality of life: local pollution has negative effects and can exacerbate the depressing nature of a neighbourhood; even basic local clean-ups can help.
- It is an excellent way of getting people involved. Taking part in a local environmental project may require nothing more than some spare energy and needn't involve technical discussions or sitting in meetings. As such it can play an important part in building stronger communities. (Church with Garratt, 2004, p 3)

The centrality of sustainable development to the 'map' of European community development can be gauged by the workshop discussion at the 2004 Budapest conference. This rested on the inseparability of community and the natural environment:"The renewal of communities and their natural environments is only possible together, according to the rules of nature. The attempt to regenerate any of them separately is doomed to failure" (Kajner, 2005: forthcoming). The workshop heard about initiatives in Hungary and Norway that illustrated the breadth of ecological politics and the key role of community development and of organisations such as CEBSD's member in Norway. The Ideas Bank has a database of examples of good practice in resource conservation, global responsibility and developing vibrant local communities and this is used both to support local action and to inform policy debates.

The way in which the Budapest workshop brought together examples, provided a forum for the sharing of ideas and agreed on a way forward in the European context illustrates how community development can engage with a new issue, linking it to both a vision for the future and a strategy for realising the vision. It is the vibrancy and energy brought to this way of working that will keep community development alive and challenging. It would be when initiatives, bold ideas and some risk taking were in short supply that warning bells should start ringing in the ears of community development organisations.

The challenge of outcomes

In one sense, community development's track record on being able to point to concrete results in its work on social exclusion is clear, specific and longstanding: reduced prices of good quality food because a food cooperative has been set up, for example; or increased incomes for poor people because local people have fought for and obtained a locally based welfare rights office. These and other kinds of initiatives have been undertaken successfully across Europe. They demonstrate the potential of community development to contribute in very practical ways to combating social exclusion. Integral to them are the principles that have been illustrated and discussed in this publication, based on the idea of supporting and organising communities to set up democratically run community groups. As part of the process of planning, action and reflection, community workers encourage members of groups to explore other avenues, especially education, training and capacity building opportunities.

Funding organisations and agencies that employ community workers, however, require more than this. They ask for evidence both on how community development has reduced social exclusion and on how it has strengthened communities. An example of the kind of outcomes being looked for is from the report of the evaluation of the community development demonstration programme in eight areas in Northern Ireland characterised by weak community infrastructure. The significant outcomes are highlighted as follows:

> *Personal empowerment*: a number of the projects had a clear focus on enhancing skills and knowledge of participants. These ranged from basic skills to vocational training. Projects have enabled individuals to embark upon a progression route from social and basic skills to more advanced accredited training that is enhancing their confidence, self-esteem and employability. In some cases this has been linked to a local employment strategy. New leaders have emerged who can play an active role in on-going community development and represent the community in other forums. This has been supported by increased community involvement in the management and operation of groups. As a result there are raised expectations and confidence of what change is possible.

> *Community organisation*: new, inclusive and participative structures have been created. Good progress has been made towards the establishment of strong, accountable and sustainable organisations with the capacity to implement planned and informed responses to local need. In many cases a new focal point was established for community life – as a resource for information, advice and guidance, a strategic coordinator, a facilitator of local groups, a locus

through which social and economic need could be tackled, and an affirmed and widely acknowledged point of contact in the area.

Positive action: a key aspect of work in this area was the adoption of inclusive approaches to participation. Significant progress was made in improving community relations and in providing for joint working across interfaces. A wide range of tools was used to promote inclusion. Community festivals and cultural activities have played a key role in developing a positive image and encouraging participation. Particular effort was made in relation to certain groups, notably young people.

Power, relationships and participation: success in this area has been significantly affected by external factors and there were both positive and negative experiences. Relationships have been developed and links established with statutory and voluntary sector organisations. Representation on strategic partnerships and wider networks has been gained and communication channels opened. The value of inter-agency approaches has been recognised, in particular by groups themselves, and some have embarked on a local policy and lobbying function. (Northern Ireland Voluntary Trust, 1999, pp 6-7)

For each of the statements made in the report, specific examples are available. The report is a useful example, therefore, of how the impact of community development can be measured and of how many of the positive outcomes relate directly to community development principles. It is a particularly relevant example here because of the demonstration programme having been initiated in areas experiencing high levels of social exclusion and weak community organisations.

We saw in Chapter Four how community development is increasingly using evaluation models – the ABCD model of the Scottish Community Development Centre and various forms of participatory action research – and it is essential for this momentum to be sustained in the European context. There are two reasons for this: on the one hand, communities themselves need to know how community development principles and methods impact on them. That, for example, is one of the messages behind the practice model developed by the Ghent group in CEBSD's project: local people want feedback on the process. Any idea that communities are somehow not living, active entities need to be challenged. In the past, there was too much of doing things to communities. Now things are done with them, and that must include feedback on outcomes.

The second, very different reason has to do with understanding the politics of European policy making, not least the competitive context in which influencing, lobbying and information-giving take place. At the Brussels conference convened by CEBSD in 2004 to discuss how to combine policy and practice, the director of the European Social Platform reminded participants of this reality:

> It is clear that business interests are much more powerful in Brussels than we are. That is why we have to work together.... At the Lisbon summit politicians committed themselves to the economy, jobs and social cohesion (in which community development is central). They remember about the economy and jobs, but they almost always forget about social cohesion – or they think of it as something that is only created by the economy and jobs rather than something larger. (Wilson, 2004)

He pointed out that community development is not included in its own right in the EU's social action programme for 2007-2113. Consequently, the case has to be made for showing that community development can bring added value to the programme. This places a major responsibility on European non-governmental organisations and networks. To gain ground with the argument for community development they need evidence on what it can achieve.

Developing standards of good practice

At the same time as it seeks to respond to external requirements to prove its worth, community development is aware that it needs to strengthen its own basis for learning. The scope for doing this within a European framework is considerable, especially with regard to training and research. Progress here would add to the basic understanding of community development across Europe investigated by Hautekeur (2004) and discussed in Chapter Five. There is an awareness within community development organisations of the need to develop standards of good practice that are both strong and authentic and are convincing not only to policy makers but also to other professions and disciplines.

CEBSD's experience of running the EU project has been a significant milestone in this respect.

On training, CEBSD plans to take forward the idea of creating a European core curriculum on community development that would be relevant to a diversity of contexts. This work would draw on the various traditions that have informed community development: community and adult education, social work, economic development and cultural work. The hope is that the idea of providing or signposting 'progression routes' for community activists, community workers, planners and others will gain wider acceptance within Europe. This would enable people to choose a level and type of learning appropriate to their experience. This long-term goal would need to be based on there being an active network for the exchange of learning in the field of community development. There is evidence that this can happen on a bilateral basis. The next step is to develop a broader European approach. It would draw on the community development literature of a number of countries as well as the more modest literature on Europe as a whole.

In a wide-ranging paper given to the workshop on research and community development at the 2004 Budapest conference, Alan Barr summarises types of research that are recognised by practitioners as making a potential contribution to their work. Using the experience of the Scottish Community Development Centre he identifies the following reasons for valuing research as a tool for practice:

- Such research is grounded in and values community experience. It treats the communities as authoritative in relation to their own needs and priorities. As a result it addresses questions that actually matter to people.

- It is designed to enhance the capacity and ability of communities and those who work with them to be architects of improvement. Informed communities with understanding of their own needs, and their competence in tackling them, become more confident and capable. Research therefore becomes a tool of empowerment. As a tool of practice it contributes greatly to learning. It not only establishes a knowledge base about the community, it also encourages and supports reflection on experience and engagement in debate with others about that experience.

- It challenges false assumptions about the objectivity of external research. It enables those who have been the objects to critically examine the way in which conventional research has constructed its perception of their experience. This is part of the empowerment process.

- As a tool of practice, research is demystified. As with all professions researchers have constructed an exclusivity about their skills that frequently denies opportunity for ordinary people to recognise their capacity to acquire and use such skills. It is of course important to recognise that there are very different levels of sophistication in research methods but it is a continuum in which much can be done that is highly beneficial without requiring great complexity. At a basic level the skills of research and enquiry are almost a natural human attribute without which we cannot conduct our lives effectively. Most people can understand what is involved and, with support, do it at a basic level. The methods that are used can be highly accessible, for example, pictorial methods of data collection.

- Research can promote equalities and inclusion. Challenging the exclusivity of research is a part of this. But it is the allying of research methods to the underlying principles of community development that encourages the use of research to understand the experience of those who are most excluded and enable them to articulate those experiences. (Barr, 2005: forthcoming)

This extract gives an idea of the scope for strengthening the research component of community development within a European framework. From this sphere of work there could be evidence-based material to add to standards of good practice. They need to be standards that have been arrived at rigorously and in an open, transparent way but they also – remembering the challenge of convincing European policy makers – need to be brought together in ways that can be communicated effectively to those outside community development as well as those within it.

Supporting new 'players'

The experience of CEBSD's project on community development and social exclusion is that not only is involving local people in working on European policy and practice effective, it is also essential: local people who have direct experience of community development are the new 'players' on the European scene. The accumulation of their various and diverse experiences in neighbourhoods and communities of interest and identity stretches back many years. Now these experiences need to be recognised and worked with at the European level. They need to be considered as normal good practice by European networks.

Clearly, there are financial and other problems raised by putting forward this objective, but these pale into insignificance compared with the problems community development would face if the idea is not taken seriously. There would be a danger that community development would ossify, losing both its sharpness and its credibility. It is crucial that the voices of local people are heard and listened to alongside the voices of community development professionals at European policy and practice conferences and other forums. The way in which this worked successfully at the meetings in Berlin and Brussels organised for all members of the groups who were part of CEBSD's project provides a useful model.

There are opportunities when local people can be directly involved in discussions with policy makers. At other times, community development organisations need people who can speak on behalf of community development, advocates who have experience of community development and who have the skills to put a case strongly in policy meetings. This relates to the more general point of the need for European community development to work at a number of different levels and in a variety of forums. Such a strategy can only be implemented if individuals and organisations undertake different roles.

Ways in which adult education institutions and community development organisations in some countries have worked with a European framework can provide guidance on how to take forward the idea of broadening participation. We referred in Chapter Two to Northern College, Barnsley, which runs residential courses for community activists; activists from Central and Eastern European countries have also participated in these. The Hungarian Association for Community Development's Civil College is a base where activists, community workers, local government staff and others in Hungary can meet to learn and share, but it is also used as a focal point for bringing together members of CEBSD and representatives of partner organisations in Central and Eastern Europe.

Crucial to strengthening this aspect of European community development is the language used to describe and explain it. The jargon and density used in papers and at conferences need to be 'unpacked' so that key points are made clearly. The objective should be to use a community development language that is both clear and accessible, based on the assumption that an important part of the job of community development is to demystify political and organisational processes. The issue of language is especially important when community development is working with the most oppressed communities because many people will be communicating in a second language.

Resources to enable local people to participate in European networks and meetings will be needed and, realistically, progress is likely to be slow. The starting point has to be a recognition across Europe of the need to make a commitment in principle to the objective.

A European commitment

All six themes that have been outlined need to form part of a vision and strategy for strengthening community development in Europe. Key to this must be the continuing commitment of national community development organisations to supporting work at the European level. Opportunities arise sometimes for expanding this area of work. For example, in the UK CDF, in partnership with Community Service Volunteers, obtained government funding to run a project aimed at ensuring that the EU's next Structural Fund programme includes clear requirements and guidelines to strengthen social capital and civil society. The results of the project will be of benefit to other member organisations of CEBSD as well as CDF.

Commitment to working at a European level can be sustained by turning to a variety of sources, from the excitement of sharing ideas and experiences at a European seminar to recalling the commitment of a handful of individuals working on behalf of their community facing exceptionally difficult circumstances; or it may be a community play in another country that captures the strong feelings held by community members, a community festival that expresses the optimism and enjoyment that can exist in communities, or simply a conversation between a visiting community worker and experienced local activists.

The importance of community development networks and organisations working closely with other European networks has been emphasised already, especially those supporting women and those working on race issues. Equally important is for community development organisations to look more closely at the potential within institutions for their resources to support community development. Universities can be particularly useful in that respect. They can be partners in a European consortium applying for funds, they can help with the development and implementation of research projects and they can keep community development informed about developing perspectives on the key ideas of social capital and civil society and new data on social exclusion and inequality.

The dynamic between theory and practice in community development is a necessary feature of this field. At their optimum, each informs and feeds off the other. Similarly, the tension between community development and social exclusion referred to in Chapter Five in the context of the discussion on the Budapest Declaration should not be interpreted as a problem but rather as a source of debate and creativity. Community development and combating social exclusion cannot exist in isolation from each other, but individuals and organisations across Europe can give them different emphasis. The objective should be to get them working off each other so that both are strengthened. This is especially important with regard to gender: the experience of women who have played key roles in community action and activities, and how they have learned and gained confidence from this, is closely aligned with the demand from women in poverty to be treated with dignity and respect.

Furthermore, those people involved in community development and in combating social exclusion share the same determination of ensuring that the voices of poor and disadvantaged people are really listened to, not managed in tokenistic ways by people in positions of power. A key point made to the UK Commission on Poverty, Participation and Power was that "people experiencing poverty see consultation without commitment, and phoney participation without the power to bring about change, as the ultimate disrespect" (Carter and Petch, 2000, p 18). Similar feelings of anger and cynicism at having been ignored or treated in an offhand way by resource-holders or decision makers can be found within some communities. It is here that the idea of good practice in community development becomes critical: ensuring that the lessons of how to work effectively and in partnership with community groups are understood and adopted by a range of professionals. The need for this is doubly important in areas where there is widespread poverty and social exclusion.

Searching for authentic forms of participation needs to be on the agendas of all organisations that seek to engage with and support deprived communities. On the one hand, this requires professionals to have a deep understanding of how to plan and have dialogue with communities, rooted in the ideas of Paulo Freire and other adult and community education theorists. On the other hand, it means testing out and adapting the many participation methods and techniques that are available (Henderson, 2003b).

Genuine participation is one of the central ideas that inform organisations' commitment to civil society: "The ability of citizens to initiate and act in the community. This goal is meant to be achieved through increasing participation of citizens in their own and in their common affairs, through improving the community-related conditions of local action, and through building-up the local institutions of democracy" (HACD, 2001, p 1).

Both communities and institutions have to change if grassroots participation is to work. If we reflect on the situations described in the seven case studies in Chapter Three, the need for participation to remain a central concern is very apparent. Both as a concept and a method, it should inform the actions of community groups so that:

- membership of groups is kept open;
- new ways of working between citizens and institutions can be proposed;
- democratic processes of society in general are strengthened.

Institutions, particularly large-scale service delivery organisations, have to engage with the issue of participation of excluded people in planning and consultation processes. They need to make stronger connections with communities and to do this they must change their structures and procedures and become more knowledgeable about the diversity of communities:

> Civil society and the citizen is the ideal for those seeking a better society.... This struggle, however, is not justified only at historical turning points such as the transformation in central and eastern Europe to a free, democratic, open society. For a variety of reasons, both the old and the new democracies need to continuously fight for a strong civil society, whether this task is the establishment of democratic institutions or the handling of the crisis symptoms of the welfare state. (Vercseg, 2005: forthcoming)

By reaffirming its commitment to building civil society and democracy, community development of necessity sets itself the challenge of responding to social exclusion. The EU project, the findings of which have formed the basis of this book, has sent out important messages as to how this can be done within a European framework. The obstacles are considerable and progress will be achieved only over a long time period. It is for this reason that the argument for putting in place some essential building blocks has been made: European networks that are open and inclusive, learning and training opportunities, alliances with issue-based and social policy non-governmental organisations, and disseminating examples of good practice and their policy implications. These resources and processes are needed if community development in Europe is to have a meaningful and significant impact.

References

Alinsky, S.D. (1972) *Rules for radicals*, New York, NY: Vintage Books.

Banks, S. (2004) 'The concept of community practice', in S. Banks, H. Butcher, P. Henderson and J. Robertson (eds) *Managing community practice*, Bristol: The Policy Press, pp 9-22.

Barr, A. (2005: forthcoming) 'The contribution of research to community development – a reflection on types, methods and experience', *Community Development Journal*.

Barr, A. and Hashagen, S. (2000) *ABCD handbook: A framework for evaluating community development*, London: CDF Publications.

Barr, A., Stenhouse, C. and Henderson, P. (2001) *Caring communities. A challenge for social inclusion*, York: Joseph Rowntree Foundation.

Bauman, Z. (2001) *Community: Seeking safety in an insecure world*, Cambridge: Polity Press.

Carter, M. and Petch, H. (2000) *Listen hear: The right to be heard*, Bristol: The Policy Press on behalf of the Commission on Poverty, Participation and Power.

CEBSD (Combined European Bureau for Social Development) (2004) 'Good practice in community development. Report of Berlin seminar', mimeo, Lageny (Ireland): CEBSD.

Chanan, G. (2004) *Measures of community*, London: CDF Publications.

Church, C. with Garratt, C. (2004) *Changing where we live*, London: CDF Publications (in association with Groundwork UK).

Civil Renewal Unit (2004) *Firm foundations: The government's framework for community capacity building*, London: Home Office.

Combat Poverty Agency (2000) *The role of community development in tackling poverty*, Dublin: Combat Poverty Agency.

Cousins, L. (2005) 'The contribution that community development can make to tackling social exclusion and poverty', mimeo, Leeds: Leeds Metropolitan University.

Craig, G., Ahmed, B. and Amery, F. (1999) '"We shoot them at Newark!" The work of the Lincolnshire Forum for Racial Justice', in P. Henderson and R. Kaur (eds) *Rural racism in the UK: Examples of community-based responses*, London: CDF Publications, pp 22-32.

Craig, G., Shucksmith, M. and Young-Smith, L. (2004) *Rural community development in Europe*, Dunfermline: Carnegie Commission for Rural Community Development.

Dalton, R. and Wattenberg, M. (2000) *Parties without partisans*, Oxford: Oxford University Press.

Demos Project (2004) *Citizens, innovation, local governance: Report and guidelines*, Edinburgh: Demos Project (www.demosproject.org).

European Council (2000) *Presidency conclusions*, Lisbon: European Council, 23/24 March.

EU (European Union) (2004) *Treaty establishing a Constitution for Europe*, Brussels, 13 October.

Forrest, R. and Kearns, A. (1999) *Joined-up places? Social cohesion and neighbourhood regeneration*, York: Joseph Rowntree Foundation.

Frazer, H. (2005: forthcoming) 'Setting the scene Europe wide: the challenge of poverty and social exclusion', *Community Development Journal*.

Gilchrist, A. (2004a) *Community cohesion and community development*, London: CDF Publications.

Gilchrist, A. (2004b) *The well-connected community: A networking approach to community development*, Bristol: The Policy Press.

Glen, A., Henderson, P., Humm, J., Meszaros, H. with Gaffney, M. (2004) *Survey of community development workers in the UK*, London: CDF Publications (with Community Development Exchange).

Gorman, M. (2003) 'European project on Good Practice in Community Development', Report to the European Commission, mimeo, Lagney (Ireland): CEBSD.

HACD (Hungarian Association for Community Development) (2001) *Annual report: Hungarian Association for Community Development*, Budapest: HACD.

Harvey, B. (2003) *The potential of local social capital in the struggle against social exclusion*, Brussels: EAPN.

Hautekeur, G. (2004) *Community development in Europe*, Brussels: CEBSD.

Henderson, P. (2003a) 'European trends in community development', seminar paper, Sovata, Romania, 27-28 March, Budapest: HACD.

Henderson, P. (2003b) *CHOICE: Examples of community participation methods*, London: CDF Publications.

Henderson, P. and Salmon, H. (2001) *Social exclusion and community development*, London: CDF Publications.

Henderson, P. and Thomas, D.N. (2002) *Skills in neighbourhood work* (3rd edn), London: Routledge.

Humm, J., Jones, K. and Chanan, G. (2004) 'Testing indicators of community involvement', Interim report, mimeo, London: CDF Publications.

Jensen, J. and Miszlivetz, F. (2003) 'The languages of civil society: Europe and beyond', draft report, mimeo: Szombathely, Hungary: CISONET.

Kajner, P. (2005: forthcoming) 'All is one: only healthy communities can build a sustainable future', *Community Development Journal.*

Katz, B. (2004) *Neighbourhoods of choice and connection*, York: Joseph Rowntree Foundation.

Keane, J. (1998) *Civil society: Old images, new visions*, Cambridge: Polity Press.

Levitas, R. (1998) *The inclusive society? Social exclusion and New Labour*, Basingstoke: Macmillan.

Lister, R. (2001) 'Foreword', in P. Henderson and H. Salmon, *Social exclusion and community development*, London: CDF Publications, pp vii-ix.

Lister, R. (2004) *Poverty*, Cambridge: Polity Press.

Mayo, M. and Taylor, M. (2001) 'Partnerships and power in community regeneration', in S. Balloch and M. Taylor (eds) *Partnership working: Policy and practice*, Bristol: The Policy Press, pp 39-56.

Ministry of Justice (2002) *Time for democracy – eight good examples*, Orebro: CESAM.

Modood, T. (1997) 'Introduction: the politics of multiculturalism in the new Europe', in T. Modood and P. Werbner (eds) *The politics of multiculturalism in the new Europe*, London: Zed Books, pp 1-25.

Murdoch, S. (2005: forthcoming) 'Community development and urban regeneration', *Community Development Journal.*

Northern Ireland Voluntary Trust (1999) *Building community infrastructure: Lessons from the Community Development Demonstration Programme*, Belfast: Community Foundation for Northern Ireland.

O'Prey, M. and Magowan, J. (2001) *Weak community infrastructure: A support priority*, Belfast: Community Foundation for Northern Ireland.

Richardson, L. and Mumford, K. (2002) 'Community, neighbourhoods, and social infrastructure', in J. Hills, J. Le Grand and D. Piachaud (eds) *Understanding social exclusion*, Oxford: Oxford University Press, pp 202-25.

Riera, C. (2005: forthcoming) 'Social policies of community development in multicultural contexts', *Community Development Journal.*

Rifkin, J. (2004) *The European dream*, Cambridge: Polity Press.

Schuringa, L. (2005) *Community work and Roma inclusion*, Ostrava: University of Ostrava.

Sen, A. (1990) 'Justice: means versus freedoms', *Philosophy and Public Affairs*, vol 19, no 2, pp 111-21.

Shucksmith, M. (2000) *Exclusive countryside? Social inclusion and regeneration in rural areas*, York: Joseph Rowntree Foundation.

Skinner, S. (1997) *Building community strengths*, London: CDF Publications.

Tonkens, E. and Duyvendak, J. W. (2003) 'Paternalism – caught between rejection and acceptance: taking care and taking control in community work', *Community Development Journal*, vol 38, no 1, pp 6-15.

Van den Hoven, R. (2002) *Opbouwwerk tussen emancipatie en beheersing: een vergelijkende studie naar praktijk van opbouwwerk in Nederland en Portugal*, The Hague: Landelijk Centrum Opbouwwerk.

Vercseg, I. (2003) 'Community development in Central-Eastern Europe', seminar paper, Sovata, Romania, 27-28 March, Budapest: HACD.

Vercseg, I. (2005) 'Community development and civil renewal in Hungary', Paper presented at annual conference of the Federation for Community Development Learning, Liverpool, 2 February.

Vercseg, I. (2005: forthcoming) 'Central and Eastern Europe in the limelight', *Community Development Journal*.

Vos, K. (2005: forthcoming) 'Community development policy and legislation: the Dutch case', *Community Development Journal*.

Wilson, D. (2004) *European social policies and community development*, Brussels: CEBSD.

The Budapest Declaration

Preamble

One hundred and thirty community workers, researchers, donors and policy-makers, and representatives from government, civil society organisations and community groups, from 33 countries across the European Union and beyond, met March 25-28 2004 at an international conference, to prepare for the accession of ten new countries to the EU. The conference – focused on *building civil society in Europe through community development* – was sponsored by the International Association for Community Development, the Combined European Bureau for Social Development, and the Hungarian Association for Community Development under the patronage of the President of Hungary.

Community development is a way of strengthening civil society by prioritising the actions of communities, and their perspectives in the development of social, economic and environmental policy. It seeks the empowerment of local communities, taken to mean both geographical communities, communities of interest or identity and communities organising around specific themes or policy initiatives. It strengthens the capacity of people as active citizens through their community groups, organisations and networks; and the capacity of institutions and agencies (public, private and non-governmental) to work in dialogue with citizens to shape and determine change in their communities. It plays a crucial role in supporting active democratic life by promoting the autonomous voice of disadvantaged and vulnerable communities. It has a set of core values/social principles covering human rights, social inclusion, equality and respect for diversity; and a specific skills and knowledge base.

Delegates attending the March 2004 Budapest conference, representing civil society organisations, governments, donor agencies and community groups, acknowledge the priority now being given by the European Union to strengthen civil society and emphasise the important role which community development can play in supporting that process and protecting the human rights of all. They request the

EU, national, regional and local governments – as appropriate – to commit themselves actively to build a socially and economically inclusive, diverse, environmentally sustainable and socially just society, and to ensure the structures, policies and mechanisms are in place to support dialogue between the EU and members states on the one hand and civil society on the other. This will require both moral and practical support for community participation, and appropriate legal, institutional and material conditions, but with specific support for community development itself.

Delegates wish to stress the importance of community development in building mechanisms to promote the inclusion of all residents of Europe – whether permanent, seeking permanency or migrant. They reject both the increasingly explicit manifestations of racism and xenophobia and the implicit racism manifested in those current immigration policies, which lend credence to the notion of 'Fortress Europe'. They also acknowledge the strengthening of social, cultural and economic life, which will be consequent on the enlargement of the EU.

Delegates wish to emphasise the importance of developing mechanisms which could facilitate the sharing of best practice both within the EU but also between the EU and those many countries and institutions outside the EU (including other European countries) where community development has played a significant role in addressing poverty and social exclusion, including in situations of conflict and peace-building. Finally, they also wish to stress the need to understand the differing ways in which poverty, social exclusion and marginalisation may impact on cultural and national minorities, on migrants and on those living in rural as well as urban areas. Delegates emphasise that the practice of community development strives to endorse and give voice to minority perspectives on policy and practice development; the distinct experience of Black and Minority Ethnic communities should be an integral part of the development of policy and practice.

A key conference objective was to agree a common statement on community development in Europe, to be directed to the EU, national governments and other key stakeholders. The following is the text of this agreed statement. The conference commends the Declaration to you and urges support for the proposals below.

- **Community development policy and legislation at European, national and local levels of government**
1. The EU Director General for Employment and Social Affairs should take the lead in publishing a cross-EU policy statement in 2005 highlighting the necessity of community development in facilitating citizen participation and in building social capital. The role of community development should explicitly be recognised in this process, and coherent and sustainable funding streams be made available through the 2007 EU Structural Funds for local, regional and European networks and through better coordination with and between independent trusts, foundations and NGOs.
2. All national governments should consider the appointment of a Minister with specific responsibility for creating and implementing community development policy, by 2006. That Minister should have a cross-departmental remit. We also ask that national governments should consider introducing a statutory responsibility for community development.
3. Regional and local authorities should publish from 2007 and implement annual action plans which outline the relevant special measures including investments, monitoring and evaluation of community development in facilitating effective citizen participation. These plans should be formulated on the basis of extensive community consultation.

- **Community development training**
4. For community development to make the most effective contribution to building civil society, the EU needs to facilitate a common framework for training and learning for community development based on core community development values, knowledge and skills, with training materials based on best practices. The development of training is at present quite uneven but good experience should be used to suit local conditions.
5. This common framework for learning and training needs to be resourced and adapted for use in each member state, based on dialogue with all stakeholders, and developed from the 'bottom up'. The common overarching framework should not be used to export any one particular political or economic perspective.
6. Learning and training for community development and for active citizenship must be part of a continuum for lifelong learning and critical reflection – from citizenship education for children and young people through to community activists and volunteers, professionals working with communities and decision-makers at

different levels. There should be pathways for progression through and across different levels of learning and training.

- **Community development theory and research**
7. More attention should be given by the EU and national governments to the process of research as a vehicle for participation and the development of research skills within communities; research should be as much a tool for communities as for policy-makers.
8. To promote ownership and mutual commitment, an active dialogue should be fostered between research and practice involving all stakeholders; this will require a greater degree of reflectiveness on the part of researchers as to how their skills can be made available to local communities.
9. Research policy at EU, national and local level should be responsive to these needs and principles and direct funding to support them.
10. The EU and national governments should build on research which has demonstrated the effectiveness of community development; and create more effective mechanisms for sharing and exchanging the findings of research relevant to the needs of local communities.

- **Community development and rural issues**
11. Rural community development should be a specific and explicit priority within national and EU community development, social and economic programmes.
12. National governments and the EU will need further to activate and sustain voluntary and community action in rural areas. This should be based on a well-developed rural infrastructure; access to services for all based on need; and effective and appropriate training and support for rural community development.
13. At the EU level, it is necessary to establish a framework for rural community worker competence standards.
14. Recognising the specific challenges facing rural communities, EU and national policies should provide incentives to rural communities to mobilise their members and their resources to address local problems, strengthening their capacities to do so. As part of this process, the EU should encourage working partnerships between communities and local authorities, and between communities themselves, and ensure that appropriate government and EU mechanisms are created to respond to local initiatives.

- **Community development and urban regeneration**

15. Whilst aiming for the common goal of an inclusive and socially just civil society, to achieve effective urban regeneration through community development, it is necessary for governments and the EU to be aware of and acknowledge differing national contexts (political, cultural, historical etc) and to respond appropriately.

16. All people in areas subject to regeneration should have the right to participation at every stage in its regeneration and future, with a special focus on socially excluded groups and those who traditionally have not had a voice in these processes.

17. Sustainable and inclusive urban regeneration requires that all involved players are open to change and accept it as a learning process; this requires that community development must play a key role in the process of regeneration.

- **Community development, sustainable development and the environment**

18. Starting from a recognition that an environmentally sustainable society cannot be built without healthy and active communities (and *vice versa*), the EU should support the production of a handbook, which identifies and disseminates good practice for sustainable, ecological development and community development efforts both within Europe and outside it.

19. The EU should provide support for the establishment of a European community development network, which can disseminate better knowledge of sustainable projects, for example through a European Ideas-bank. The Bank should map experiences and support information exchange in ways, which will enable it to reach a broad public.

20. The EU or member states, as appropriate, should extend financial support in particular to local projects, which seek to integrate sustainable ecological, social, economic and community development.

- **Community development, lifelong learning and cultural development**

21. Adult education should extend beyond vocational training and should be seen as a right and provided on a non-commercial, not-for-profit basis.

22. Lifelong learning should be defined in policies as including community-based and citizenship education. By a community-based model, we mean building on local skills, resources, strengths

and needs, and recognising issues of gender, cultural diversity, sustainable development and inclusion; in short, offering 'access to diversity and diversity of access'.

23. There is a continued need for experimentation, within a secure and sustainable funding framework at local, national and EU levels. This implies a commitment to medium and long-term funding and provision. Programmes such as Grundtvig should be further developed with increased budgets and should prioritise transnational mobility for community activists and local groups alongside community development professionals.

- **Community development, local economic development and the social economy**

24. Every national action plan – including plans to combat poverty and social exclusion – should be required to include a section, which addresses the role of the social economy and local community economic development.

25. The EU should seek to disseminate existing experiences and practice both from within the EU and from outside it; networking of this social economy experience should be stimulated and supported within the EU with a specific focus on the acceding countries and those seeking accession in the near future.

26. Local communities should be recognised as active and legitimate partners in the development of plans, structures and policies for local economic development.

- **Community development, minorities, migration, racism and discrimination**

While all of the issues listed above need to focus on the needs of differing minorities, there are also additional specific issues related to their needs.

27. The EU should ensure free movement of all EU citizens accompanied by social protection, promote cohesion and solidarity for host communities, migrants and communities of origin, and combat racism and discrimination in all its forms.

28. In support of these goals, the EU and member states should create and support structures and agencies, which pursue the aims of racial equality and cross-cultural understanding and awareness. The EU and member states should at the same time emphasise the positive aspects of a wider and more diverse Europe.

29. The EU and member states should acknowledge, through policy and funding development, that community development has a critical role to play in engaging people in increasingly diverse communities through inclusive methods. This may be done by building bridges between majority and minority communities, including in situations of conflict.

30. The EU, national governments, donors and community development organisations and agencies need to work collaboratively to promote cross-border and national co-operation in relation to the position of minorities and the particular challenges they face within specific local contexts.

Combined European Bureau for Social Development

The Board Members of CEBSD are national or regional community development organisations from Belgium, Denmark, France, Germany, Hungary, Ireland, the Netherlands, Norway, Spain, Sweden and the UK. Members share information, exchange ideas and engage in training and research in community and social development.

CEBSD runs European projects, training, conferences and seminars. It is a member of the European Social Platform and works in partnership with other European and international networks such as EAPN and the International Association for Community Development. Members are committed to making the links between policy, research and practice in community development especially in the fields of social inclusion, poverty, citizens' participation and civil society.

Work on the theme of building civil society in Europe through community development produced the Budapest Declaration in the year of European enlargement (2004). The community workers, researchers, donors and policy makers from government, civil society organisations and community groups, whose aspirations are presented in the Declaration, continue to work together across Europe.

For further information on CEBSD's activities, publications and on how to access CEBSD's information exchange, visit the website at www.cebsd.org and/or contact one of the people listed later in this appendix. You can also contact CEBSD's coordinator, Margo Gorman: tel: +353 749 723129; e-mail: margogorman@eircom.net

Examples of exchange

Dialogue with Communities was a partnership event in Scotland in June 2004 designed to strengthen links between policy and practice in citizens' participation. Participants explored how they can work towards achieving a relationship between communities and the agencies that serve them, which is based on dialogue and on the prerequisites for dialogue. These were defined as information, respect, listening and learning.
www.scdc.org.uk

Community Development in Europe was a workshop held in Copenhagen in 2003. It contributed to a process of exchange, research and publication on European trends in the theoretical basis for community development and the reflection of this in training for community workers.
www.viboso.be
www.settlementet.dk

Publications

Copies of the following publications cost 10 euros each. They can be ordered from Margo Gorman: margogorman@eircom.net

Guide to equality and the EU

This guide was launched by the Equality Authority in Dublin in 2002. Written by Brian Harvey, the guide outlines current policies on equality and discrimination issues in the EU; identifies the principal agencies, institutions and monitoring bodies involved; outlines the main funding programmes concerned with equality and discrimination; locates the principal information sources on equality and discrimination issues.

The guide is available from the Equality Authority, 2 Clonmel Street, Dublin 2, Ireland. Tel: +353 1 4173333; e-mail: info@equality.ie

The neighbourhood economy at work

This bilingual publication (English and French) was inspired by a two-day European event on the neighbourhood economy in Brussels and Ghent, organised by VIBOSO and CEBSD. The publication explores concrete case studies where new forms of work have been created in neighbourhoods. By establishing local neighbourhood services, social contacts and networks are reinforced in increased social cohesion. The publication has three underlying themes:

1. participation and empowerment
2. partnership
3. financing and management.

There are contributions from several countries and the contributions cover practical experience, research and analysis.

Alcantara – building bridges between cultures

This publication presents some of the experience of the Alcantara project in Barcelona on intercultural mediation and analyses it from the perspective of community development in Europe. The material is an unusual mix of experience and ideas. Often, tension and conflict in intergroup relations are either presented negatively or with a superficial multicultural gloss. This publication goes further as it explores both intellectual and emotional dimensions of methods of resolving such tensions and conflicts.

Neighbourhood democracy at work

This report is on an exchange of ideas and experiences held in Orebro, Sweden in 2000. It was organised by CESAM in collaboration with the Swedish Association of Housing Companies and CEBSD. The report includes lectures and descriptions of neighbourhood democracy projects in Orebro and Bradford, UK.

Setting the scene: community-based responses to urban deprivation in five European countries

This report contains the presentations given at a major conference called No Europe Without Us, which was held in The Hague in 1997. It explores the commitment of agencies to the community participation dimension of urban regeneration. The contributions are from France, Germany, the Netherlands, Spain and the UK.

CEBSD contacts

Belgium: Gerard Hautekeur
VIBOSO
tel: +32 2 2010565
g.hautekeur@viboso.be
www.viboso.be

Denmark: Johannes Bertelsen
Kristeligt Studenter-Settlement (KSS)
tel: +45 33 228820
bertelsen@settlementet.dk
www.settlementet.dk

France: Marie-Renée Bourget-Daitch
Le Mouvement pour un Développement Social Local
(MDSL)
contact through Margo Gorman

Germany: Dr Armin Kuphal
Paritaetisches Bildungswerk Rheinland Pfalz/Saarland
tel: +49 681 85909 10
a.kuphal@rz.uni-sb.de
www.gemeinwesenarbeit.de

Hungary: Ilona Vercseg
Hungarian Association for Community Development
tel/fax: +36 1 2015728
vercseg@kkpcsolat.hu
www.adata.hu

Ireland: Liz Sullivan, Donald McDonald
Combat Poverty Agency
tel: +353 16 706746
sullivanL@cpa.ie
donald.mcdonald@cpa-adm.com
www.cpa.ie

The Netherlands: Fred Stafleu
Landelijk Centrum Opbouwwerk (LCO)
tel: +31 70 3804431
fred.stafleu@planet.nl
www.opbouwwerk.nl

Norway: Kirsten Paaby
The Ideas Bank
tel: +47 22 97 98 62
kirsten@idebanken.no
www.idebanken.no

Spain: Carles Riera
Desenvolupament Comunitari
tel: +34 93 2680477
criera@aepdc.es

Sweden: Hans Andersson
CESAM
tel: +46 19 17 0750
hans.andersson@cesam.se
www.cesam.se

UK: Sarah Benioff
CDF
tel: +44 207 226 5375
sarah@cdf.org.uk
www.cdf.org.uk

Coordinator: Margo Gorman
tel: +353 749 723129
margogorman@eircom.net

Consultant: Paul Henderson
tel: +44 193 7842497
henderson_ecd@yahoo.co.uk

Index

The well-connected community
A networking approach to community development
Alison Gilchrist

"In the context of contemporary policies for participation and partnership working, networking is more evidently important than ever. This book will be invaluable for community practitioners and trainers as well as for students and academics in this field." *Marjorie Mayo, Centre for Urban and Community Research, Goldsmiths College, University of London*

Paperback £18.99 US$29.95 ISBN 1 86134 527 5
234 x 156mm 176 pages January 2004

East Enders
Family and community in East London
Katharine Mumford and Anne Power

"... a useful resource for students and others wishing for a comprehensive overview of the issues facing communities and the many aspects of family life that are influenced by neighbourhood environments and interactions."
Housing Studies

Paperback £19.99 US$32.50 ISBN 1 86134 497 X
Hardback £50.00 US$75.00 ISBN 1 86134 496 1
240 x 172mm 328 pages May 2003
CASE Studies on Poverty, Place and Policy

Poverty Street
The dynamics of neighbourhood decline and renewal
Ruth Lupton

"... an excellent summary of the issues, debates and dilemmas surrounding neighbourhood renewal and decline." *Urban Studies*

Paperback £21.99 US$35.00 ISBN 1 86134 535 6
Hardback £50.00 US$79.95 ISBN 1 86134 536 4
240 x 172mm 256 pages November 2003
CASE Studies on Poverty, Place and Policy

To order further copies of this publication or any other Policy Press titles please visit **www.policypress.org.uk** or contact:

In the UK and Europe:
Marston Book Services, PO Box 269,
Abingdon, Oxon, OX14 4YN, UK
Tel: +44 (0)1235 465500
Fax: +44 (0)1235 465556
Email: direct.orders@marston.co.uk

In the USA and Canada:
ISBS, 920 NE 58th Street, Suite 300,
Portland, OR 97213-3786, USA
Tel: +1 800 944 6190 (toll free)
Fax: +1 503 280 8832
Email: info@isbs.com

In Australia and New Zealand:
DA Information Services, 648 Whitehorse Road
Mitcham, Victoria 3132, Australia
Tel: +61 (3) 9210 7777
Fax: +61 (3) 9210 7788
E-mail: service@dadirect.com.au

Further information about all of our titles can be found on our website.

07/1901/9
£ 13.34

Also available from The Policy Press

On the margins of inclusion
Changing labour markets and social exclusion in London
David Smith

"In the plethora of books and reports dealing with social exclusion/inclusion this book stands out. The sensitive and intelligent ethnography allows the outer London working class to speak for themselves and shows how social and economic change intersects with their lives. For anyone who wants to understand how people live in a post-industrial global city, this book is a must read." *David Byrne, Department of Sociology and Social Policy, University of Durham*

Paperback £21.99 US$35.00 ISBN 1 86134 600 X
Hardback £55.00 US$79.95 ISBN 1 86134 601 8
234 x 156mm 224 tbc pages September 2005
Studies in Poverty, Inequality and Social Exclusion series

Community development (Revised 2nd edition)
A critical approach
Margaret Ledwith

"This is a wonderfully readable and thoughtful book that merges theory and practice in challenging social inequality - the late Paulo Freire's central concern. Margaret Ledwith's long experience in community work underlies the vitality and insight in this new edition. For studying community needs, and for the future of 'those-not-yet-in-power', Ledwith's new edition is essential reading." *Professor Ira Shor, City University of New York Graduate School, USA*

Paperback £18.99 US$29.95 ISBN 1 86134 695 6
Hardback £55.00 US$74.50 ISBN 1 86134 696 4
234 x 156mm 144 tbc pages November 2005
A BASW/Policy Press title

Managing community practice
Principles, policies and programmes
Edited by Sarah Banks, Hugh L. Butcher, Paul Henderson and Jim Robertson

"This fine volume is further confirmation of the growing importance of 'neighbourhood' in delivering public services. The book is for managers and practitioners and helps understand 'going local' and how it will help reshape organisations as they redirect their energies toward providing neighbourhood-based services." *Community Care*

Paperback £17.99 US$28.00 ISBN 1 86134 356 6
234 x 156mm 208 pages March 2003